Contents

Introduction

A greenhouse is like a window on another world. It opens up a whole new dimension to gardening that can be completely absorbing and fulfilling — a sanctuary for the keen amateur who refuses to lay dormant during the coldest months. A greenhouse is like your very own time-machine, shifting the seasons and changing the environment for the benefit of plants. It can be a tropical bubble, or a temperate room, a blaze of colour with a bounty of fruit and vegetables. In short, it's an escape.

The key to success when using a greenhouse is equally compelling: make it fun. The moment a greenhouse becomes a chore it's a failure and the once enthusiastic beginner is turned into a disillusioned cynic vowing never to set foot inside a greenhouse again. Making greenhouse gardening fun is easy. That is, if you make life in the greenhouse easy it will be fun. Remember that any compromise made when setting up a greenhouse may seem small at the time, but will become increasingly annoying as seasons pass by.

A greenhouse is a long-term investment that will provide long-term employment with many years of exciting discoveries and achievements. There is one big advantage of not having a greenhouse though — all the excitement of setting up and embarking on the adventure of growing plants under glass for the very first time is yet to come.

Fig 1 Colourful pot plants are suitable for growing in a greenhouse.

GREENHOUSE GARDENING

Step by Step to Growing Success

Jonathan Edwards

CROWOOD GARDENING GUIDES

First published in 1988 by
The Crowood Press Ltd
Gipsy Lane, Swindon
Wiltshire SN2 6DQ

© The Crowood Press Ltd 1988, 1991

Paperback edition 1989, reprinted 1990, this revised edition published 1991

British Library Cataloguing in Publication Data

Edwards, Jonathan
  Greenhouse Gardening
  1. Trees
  1. Title
  635'.0483   SB415

ISBN 1 85223 091 6(HB), 1 85223 383 4(PB), 1 85223 575 6 (Revised edition PB)

Dedication: To Mum and Dad

Picture Credits
All photographs by Dave Pike
All colour artwork by Claire Upsdale-Jones
Cover photography courtesy of the Garden Picture Library (front: Steven Wooster, back top: Gary Rogers and back bottom: John Glover).

Readers should note that in order to make the text appropriate to both hemispheres the following guide is offered:

Month	Northern hemisphere	Southern hemisphere
January	Mid-winter	Mid-summer
February	Late winter	Late summer
March	Early spring	Early autumn
April	Mid-spring	Mid-autumn
May	Late spring	Late autumn
June	Early summer	Early winter
July	Mid-summer	Mid-winter
August	Late summer	Late winter
September	Early autumn	Early spring
October	Mid-autumn	Mid-spring
November	Late autumn	Late spring
December	Early winter	Early summer

Typeset by Avonset, Midsomer Norton, Bath
Printed and bound by Times Publishing Group, Singapore

CHAPTER 1

Choosing a Greenhouse

Greenhouses are better value today than ever before: a standard 8×6ft (2.5×1.8m) aluminium model is available at low prices everywhere from the garden centre to the high street supermarket. Having said that, a word of caution, if your choice is governed by price alone you will almost certainly live to regret it. Do not buy in haste.

If this purchase is your first greenhouse then you may well find the specifications from competing manufacturers bewildering. You need to make a checklist of your own requirements and see how each model on offer stands up.

WHAT SHAPE IS MOST SUITABLE?

As a first-time buyer of a greenhouse, the shape might not seem all that important apart from the obvious aesthetic consideration. However, the shape you choose should be determined by the types of crops you intend growing. For instance, if you are looking forward to growing the standard range of spring and summer crops like tomatoes and cucumbers then a straight-sided house is perfectly adequate. If, on the other hand you want to extend this rather limited growing season and utilize your greenhouse throughout the year then a better choice would be a model with sloping sides because they allow greater light transmission during the critical winter months.

Rather smart glass domes are now available and are ideal for the low-growing winter crops like lettuce or displays of prize alpines on staging, but this type of greenhouse doesn't afford any real growing space for taller crops like tomatoes and cucumbers.

WHAT SIZE SHOULD I BUY?

Size is determined by finances and available space. If you are a beginner taking your first tentative steps into greenhouse gardening then choose a wide, short greenhouse that can be added to as needs and ready cash allow. Check, though, that the model you buy can be added to using extension modules.

If you intend doing some serious greenhouse gardening then buy the biggest you can afford — it's even worth doing without some of the accessories for a couple of seasons to get that extra couple of feet of growing space. Where expense is no object work out the area needed to grow the intended crops, then add on a little bit extra for good measure.

Where garden space is the limiting factor, then a lean-to model is worth considering, but do site it against a sunny wall unless you intend growing ferns.

IS GLASS BETTER THAN PLASTIC?

Plastic is a recent innovation that hasn't really caught on amongst the gardening fraternity. Although a pretty conservative crowd, gardeners

Fig 2   An aluminium greenhouse.

Fig 3   A greenhouse with a three-sided wooden bottom section.

will soon take up anything that has significant advantages over the competition. So how do these two materials compare?

Well, they are pretty equal as regards light transmission, though plastic allows more infra-red light to pass in which warms the greenhouse quickly, but, conversely, lets it out just as fast and so cools down more rapidly, too. Plastic is lighter and needs smaller and fewer supporting bars. It can be curved round to make the heating area smaller without reducing the growing area and is, of course, a lot cheaper than glass. But it does attract dirt by static electricity, is degraded by sunlight so that it becomes brittle and worst of all needs replacing every few years. Even when new it is prone to splitting or puncturing by careless hands.

The   double-skinned   box-section   polycar-

Fig 4   Wooden-framed greenhouse but with the wooden bottom section replaced by glass.

bonate sheeting, on the other hand, is a very strong plastic alternative with an inherent flexibility which makes it the ideal material for anyone plagued by children using the greenhouse for target practice. It is, however, comparatively expensive, but does afford good insulation so much of the investment can be recouped in reduced heating bills.

WHICH HAS MORE TO OFFER: WOOD OR ALUMINIUM?

Aluminium is the most common material used for the greenhouse structure these days. It does not deteriorate with time and so is practically maintenance free. The ingenious design of the framework makes the aluminium greenhouse remarkably strong while still remaining lightweight. It is relatively cheap when compared to its wooden counterparts and is easy to glaze – although aluminium structures can be complicated to put together if you choose a cheap self-assembly model.

Unfortunately, since it is a metal, aluminium is a poor insulator and tends to conduct expensive heat outside, which can be a problem during early spring. This rapid cooling results in condensation forming on the inside of the greenhouse that encourages disease problems. However, condensation can to some extent be eliminated by insulating the structure.

Greenhouses made from softwood are competitively priced and look attractive in the garden

7

Fig 5   A round aluminium greenhouse.

setting. The softwood structure does, though, have one significant disadvantage in that it is prone to rotting and needs treating regularly with a wood preservative. This is not only a chore but can be a hazardous occupation, particularly on the wider span models. However, with the advent of pressure-treated timber and the introduction of plant-safe preservatives these disadvantages are reduced. Wood also insulates and so is cheaper to heat.

Fig 6   A round wooden greenhouse.

If well made, a wooden structure is flexible enough to support a range of shelves and wires without extra strengthening. Pins can be pushed into the wood allowing quick and easy partition-ing with plastic sheeting or the straightforward erection of insulation and shading. Aluminium greenhouses need complex and often expensive clips to achieve the same result.

Cedar is expensive. If you can afford it, though, buy it. It's not too expensive to heat, is a good

Fig 7 An aluminium lean-to.

such as grey mould. Unfortunately, many cheaper models fall short in this regard and to have extra ventilation put in can increase the price considerably. Look for one roof vent (or preferably two) and two low-level side vents in a 6×8ft (1.8×2.5m) greenhouse.

Standard hinged, louvred or sliding vents all work adequately. On the side of a greenhouse, however, hinged vents can be a safety hazard. Louvres are draughty in winter and sliding vents have an annoying habit of getting stuck. Aim to have vents on both sides of the greenhouse so that at least one can be opened on the leeward side on windy days.

WHAT ABOUT ACCESS?

Both sliding and hinged doors are available. Sliding doors take less space and can be easily secured in a partially opened position for added ventilation. However, the runners are liable to become clogged and the nylon wheels do sometimes need replacing. Hinged doors need little maintenance apart from a little oil now and again, but they can restrict access, particularly if the door opens inwards. With all doors, though, make sure they are wide enough to get in and out of the greenhouse with a wheelbarrow otherwise the movement of materials will be a laborious task of carrying to and fro.

ARE THERE ANY HIDDEN EXTRAS?

There are a few manufacturers who are inclined to make essential equipment like vents and greenhouse bases an addition to the basic price. Delivery charges and erection costs can, in some cases, inflate the price out of all recognition.

Check carefully as to what is included in the price before you buy and obtain a written estimate for the basic price and all the extras involved. The best advice of all, though, is to shop around.

insulator and doesn't suffer from the dreaded condensation. Since cedar is inherently rot resistant it needs little maintenance. A preservation treatment every few years will keep it looking in tip-top condition.

HOW MUCH VENTILATION DO I NEED?

Plants grown in greenhouses need proper ventilation to prevent the spread of fungal diseases

CHAPTER 2

Siting a Greenhouse

It doesn't matter how good your greenhouse is or how green your fingers, if your greenhouse is sited in the wrong place (for instance, under overhanging trees) results will inevitably be disappointing.

LIGHT

Good light is essential – preferably on an open site well away from fences, buildings and overhanging greenery. If the available light is reduced, then the crop yields will be diminished.

Furthermore, in autumn deciduous trees very often create an additional problem with falling leaves blocking the gutters and drain-pipes. Trees also harbour pests and diseases that need no invitation to plague your greenhouse crops. Some trees such as lime will even spatter your house with a sticky exudate that is soon colonized by a spreading sheet of algae and moulds.

SHELTER

Although the best light may well be on top of a nearby mountain or hill this is probably the last place you want to site your greenhouse. The exposure, if not destructive, would certainly curtail crop yields and increase heating costs considerably!

In effect a balance is needed: away from shade, but sheltered from the worst of the weather.

FROST POCKETS

Frost pockets can be found behind walls or dense evergreen hedges at the bottom of a slope. They are trapped cold air that has run down the slope and been caught by the solid barrier. Don't erect your greenhouse in such a position.

MAIN SERVICES

Supplying water and electricity services to a greenhouse can add considerably to its initial cost. Although desirable, it is not essential to have either. However, it is worth noting that a greenhouse without these services will have limited use. After all, the easier a job the far more likely it is to get done.

If you want these services then they should be a prime consideration when you are deciding on a site since the further a greenhouse is from the mains supply the more costly the installation.

ACCESS

Just as a new town needs good road links to prosper, so a new greenhouse needs to have weather-proof pathways and be conveniently sited. If it is at the bottom of the garden at the end of a long, narrow, muddy path then it will, at best, become a fairweather hobby.

Best of all, site your greenhouse a few yards from the back door with a clean, even paved access path to it and right around it.

ORIENTATION

Much confusing advice is available about which way to point your greenhouse for best results. For general purpose growing the apex of the greenhouse should run north–south, but if you intend cultivating winter crops that need a lot of light then it is better to position it with the apex running east–west. This argument, though, tends to be rather academic since most small gardens do not provide enough space to afford the luxury of choosing direction. The difference it makes is rather marginal anyway, except with a particularly long, narrow greenhouse.

FOUNDATIONS

Laying good foundations makes greenhouse construction a simple job. Many models are available with ready-made bases (sometimes as an optional extra) that consist of pre-cast concrete kerbstones which fit accurately together to form a rectangle. These usually require setting in the ground to a depth of a couple of inches (5cm) or so. Check that the corners are exactly square using a 3, 4, 5, triangle before firming in the soil. (A triangle of sides 3, 4, and 5 units (inches, metres, etc) gives an accurate 90° angle.) Also, on exposed sites, further anchorage may be necessary so consult your dealer.

GLAZING

Always glaze your greenhouse after erection. Many models come with glass cut to size and ready to be slotted into position, but others need glazing. Use horticultural quality glass, that is, 3mm or 24oz panes.

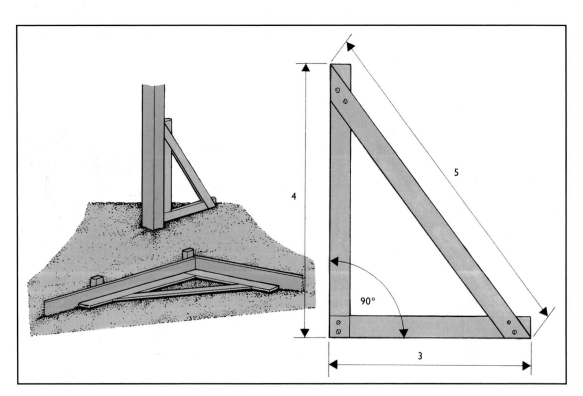

Fig 8   Using a 3, 4, 5 triangle.

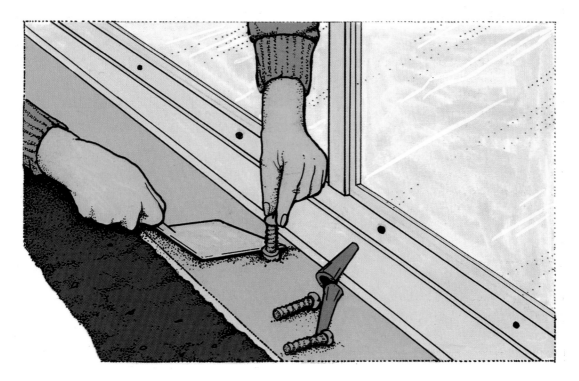

Fig 9   On exposed sites further anchorage may be necessary.

Fig 10   The base of the greenhouse plays an important part in the
levelling of the greenhouse.

Fig II   The base of a greenhouse enlarged.

Aluminium greenhouses are usually easy to glaze using plastic or rubber bedding strips set in the glazing bars. All you need to do is position the glass and snap in a few glazing clips and the job is done.

Wooden structures can be more of a problem, involving the traditional and rather messy business of setting glass on putty and holding with glazing sprigs.

With all types of glazing where the panes overlap, remember to start at the bottom and work upwards otherwise when the inevitable rains come the overlaps won't shed water, but collect it!

14

CHAPTER 3

Greenhouse Equipment

HEATING

Some form of heating is essential if you are to get the most out of your greenhouse. Don't be put off by talk of daunting bills and winter losses. All you need to do is choose the right heater for your greenhouse, situation and the crop you are growing, then simply take steps to stop the precious heat escaping.

There are five basic types of greenhouse heater: those that use solid fuel, paraffin, bottled propane, natural gas and electricity. Each type has its own advantages and disadvantages and which you choose will largely depend on the availability of fuel supply.

Fig 12   Paraffin heaters are a good back-up system.

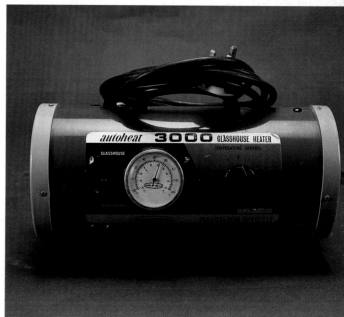

Fig 13   Electricity is a clean and simple form of heating.

Soil-heating Cables

Heating the entire greenhouse for the sake of a few overwintering plants doesn't make economic sense. It is far better to make or buy a smaller frame and fit it out with bottom heat. Soil-warming cables in a small frame can maintain a frost-free temperature for just one or two units each day even during the coldest months. If you are using Economy 7 power then this cost will be very low indeed.

15

Fig 14 *Soil-warming cables are easy to install in frame or greenhouse border.*

Soil-warming cables are available in several different lengths. Which one you choose will depend on the area you want to heat and the minimum temperature you want to achieve.

Insulation

The value of fitting insulation will entirely depend on the location of your greenhouse and the crops you intend growing. If you're on an exposed spot in the north and you want to grow early tomatoes, then the money spent on even the most expensive insulation would be recouped in a matter of weeks. But if you are just keeping the frost out in a sheltered corner in the south then it may take you a lifetime to get your money's worth. On average, though, you can expect a saving of up to 45 per cent on the cost of heating 6×8ft (1.8×2.5m) greenhouse.

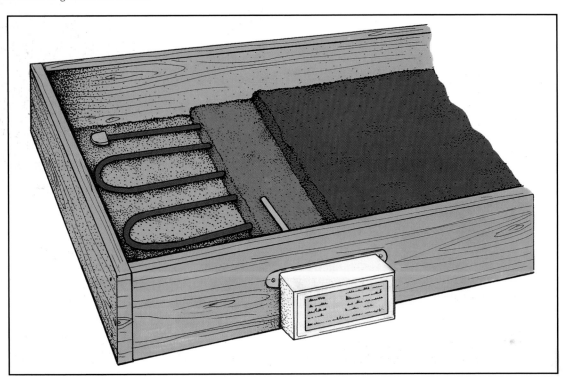

Fig 15 *A rod thermostat should be fitted at right angles to the direction of the soil-warming cable loops.*

When fitting your insulation make sure the vents are left free of obstruction. Where combustible fuels are being used you will need air movement all winter and, even with electricity, ventilation is essential on those bright spring days when the greenhouse heats up so rapidly.

Low-cost Heating

1 Choose a sheltered site for your greenhouse.
2 Heat and insulate the minimum area necessary by partitioning off a portion of the greenhouse.
3 Choose the right heater for your situation.
4 Heat only when necessary – an extra 5° can double your fuel bills.
5 Draughtproof your greenhouse making sure, though, that the vents remain obstruction free.
6 Insulate.

SHADING

There are many sun-loving plants the beginner can grow that will lap up the all too brief spells of sunshine in a wet climate. There may be only two or three months in an average year when shading is really necessary; the rest of the time temperature can be controlled by damping down and careful ventilation.

A beginner can avoid a lot of the need for shading by giving a little thought to the layout of a greenhouse; put those sun-worshipping plants like tomatoes on the south side and the rest on the north side where they will thrive in the shade of their taller neighbours. Still, this won't be enough during the hottest months, particularly if it's a scorching summer. The amount of shading you need, therefore, is dependent on the types of plants you grow. But there are also other factors to consider, including where you live, not just how far north, but at what altitude, as well as the situation and condition of your greenhouse. If it's in the shadow of something or has dirty glass then less shading will be required.

Fig 16(a)–(c) Proprietary whitewashes are applied directly to the glass.

Fig 16b(above) and Fig 16c(below).

Suitable Shading

Don't forget if you intend to use shading to keep down the temperature. It should be on the outside of the glass because when light energy hits the shading it is changed to heat energy that, if on the inside, cannot escape the confines of the greenhouse – the magical 'greenhouse effect'. However, in exposed windy spots external blinds may not stay in place long enough to give any protection at all!

VENTILATION

To keep the greenhouse temperature at an optimum level during the spring and summer it is necessary to have some form of ventilation. Even during frosty mornings in spring, sunlight energy spears its way into the greenhouse where it turns to heat energy on coming into contact with soil or staging. This lower frequency heat energy is then unable to escape from the greenhouse, rapidly increasing the temperature of the soil and air.

There are a range of ventilators on the market and available to the greenhouse gardener of which the hinged roof vent is probably the most common and found in many of the cheaper greenhouses. Alternatively, some manufacturers offer hinged side vents, but to get a good through draught of air you'll need both types and preferably more than one of each. Side-mounted hinge vents can be a safety hazard with children, so the flush louvre vents might be more practical. Louvre vents also give better air circulation than the hinged type, but tend to be less draughtproof when closed.

Sliding vents are available on some models of greenhouse and work wonderfully until a

Fig 17 Shading helps to control the temperature within the greenhouse.

Fig 18 Ventilation slats help to control the air flow and therefore the temperature inside the greenhouse.

dastardly piece of grit or sticky lump of mud gets lodged in the runner.

Opening and closing vents becomes a real bore after just a few days and so some form of automatic vent opener is a worthwhile investment. There are a good many makes available but they all operate on the same principle: the heat from the sun causes the wax contained in a cylinder to expand. This forces a piston out which, via some form of adjustable hinged lever system, then opens the vent. When the wax cools it contracts allowing the piston to be pushed back into the cylinder causing the vent to close.

Fig 19 Automatic vent openers are a good investment.

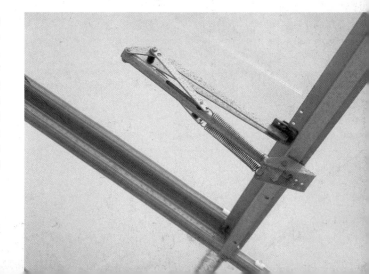

STAGING

To maximize the room in your greenhouse it's worth investing in staging. Whether wood or aluminium, purpose-built or home-made, it must be strong. Although many of the rigours to which staging is subjected are lightweight like potting and taking cuttings, in the spring it will be stacked high with plants and heavy with seedtrays – not to mention a propagator and maybe even an automatic watering system.

All staging needs a firm footing to avoid disaster. Make sure the back legs are set solid in the outside wall foundations of the greenhouse and the front on the central path base. If you are making staging remember to get the height exactly right – a few inches too high or too low will soon give you backache.

Maintenance-free aluminium staging is becoming more popular and comes in many shapes and sizes, makes and styles. Some are available with reversible trays to make a flat standing surface which can be removed for easy plant handling.

Other forms of staging are designed to fold away when not in use – very useful in spring when the staging is overflowing with seedlings. Shelving is also a useful addition to the greenhouse to increase growing space.

PROPAGATORS

To a gardener a propagator is nearly as good as money in the bank. It makes it possible to sow seed in the depths of winter with the minimum of fuss and at little cost. In addition, a propagator increases the range of plants you are able to grow by providing the high temperature environment needed to germinate some of the more exotic species of plants.

The added flexibility a propagator gives the greenhouse gardener should also not be overlooked – helping bring on slow germinating subjects as well as enabling the more forgetful of us to sow seed a little later than normally recommended.

Fig 20 Wooden staging.

Fig 2l(a) and (b)   Free-standing aluminium staging is becoming popular and foldaway staging is a real boon during the spring.

Fig 22   The cheapest propagators are useful for germinating small amounts of seeds.

The simplest form of propagator is basically a seedtray with a heating pad in its base – the better ones come supplied with a clear plastic lid with adjustable ventilation holes. This is perfectly adequate for germinating the majority of seed offered and is particularly useful if used in conjunction with the quarter-size trays that fit snugly inside. You can then sow four different seeds at once without having to worry about their varying rates of germination. Apart from its small size, the main drawback of this type of propagator is the lack of temperature control. Although the heating pad gives out a consistent heat, the actual temperature achieved will fluctuate according to the surrounding environmental temperature.

The versatile thermostatically regulated propagators cost more, but the extra control they afford over the environment makes successful seed germination a little less hit and miss. They tend to be larger too.

Propagators are also ideal for rooting cuttings – offering a constant bottom heat to encourage rooting while keeping the atmosphere humid, so preventing the leafy tops from flagging.

If you intend to overwinter plants in a propagator and thus save on greenhouse heating bills then consider buying one with a high top – this will provide the necessary growing space.

Anyone without an electricity supply in their greenhouse can buy a paraffin-heated propagator. This is basically a small paraffin heater that stands underneath a galvanized table. This heats up, keeping the seedlings standing on top in a cosy environment. However, careful ventilation would be a good idea to prevent the fumes given off by the heater harming the emerging seedlings.

WATERING

Watering with a fine-rosed watering can is by far the most reliable way of irrigating your plants, provided you can spare the time and have the energy to carry water around all day long. There

capillary watering

hand watering

gravity-fed semi-automatic irrigation

watering computer

trickle irrigation

Fig 23 *Different watering methods.*

won't be time either for holidays or even weekends away from the hustle and bustle of watering a greenhouse by hand. Of course, all this time spent in the greenhouse holding a watering can isn't entirely wasted because you can take the opportunity of studying each and every plant at close quarters. Check for pests, diseases, sideshoots, flowerbuds and developing fruits, this enables quick action when problems occur.

There are many watering systems available to reduce plants' dependence on gardeners. Some are partially automatic — with reservoirs which need topping up regularly — and there is now a trend towards completely independent, computer-operated systems that can be left alone once set up except for a few checks each week.

LIGHTING

It is no secret that plants need light in order to grow and prosper. In the summer this isn't a problem with natural light levels far exceeding the plants' requirements even on dull and overcast days. In the winter, however, it's quite a different story. Light levels on bleak mid-January days can be too low for some plants to survive, and the short day length does nothing to relieve this problem.

Supplementary lighting is the remedy. String up a series of growing lamps to supplement low light levels and extend the day length. The latter is particularly important with some plants, like

Fig 24 Supplementary lighting provides the sort of light plants require.

chrysanthemums, that need specific periods of light and dark before they will produce flowerbuds.

Unfortunately, any old lightbulb will not satisfy the plants' needs — ordinary household bulbs emit only part of the light spectrum that plants require, so special growing bulbs are needed. Several manufacturers supply specially designed bulbs for plants, indoors and outside in the greenhouse.

CHAPTER 4

Composts and Containers

COMPOSTS

To a novice, choosing a compost can be one of the most confusing aspects of greenhouse gardening. It is the life-support medium for all container-grown plants, so it's worth spending a little time to understand the fundamentals.

Years ago professional gardeners would take great pride in their composts, altering the composition to suit every plant in the garden. Unfortunately, this took a lifetime's experience to get right and these composts became some of the gardener's most closely guarded secrets. It was a very wasteful method of growing with trial and error experiments being performed up and down the country by countless individuals trying to achieve the same result.

The John Innes Horticultural Institute, therefore, decided to set up a series of scientifically controlled experiments to develop a range of standard composts that would pander to the needs of all container-grown plants. After a long series of experiments they came up with a range of composts: John Innes seed compost (J.I.S.) for sowing, and three potting composts containing varying amounts of fertilizer to suit the demands of different plants.

John Innes No. I is for potting up seedlings into their first 3½in (9cm) pot (it can also be used for sowing strong growing plants such as sweet peas). John Innes No. 2 is for potting the majority of plants and John Innes No. 3 for demanding plants such as tomatoes. Formulated over fifty years ago, these mixtures are still going strong.

Loam-based Composts

John Innes composts come in a wide range of sizes from a host of manufacturers. It is not a brand name but simply a recipe used to produce a recognized product. Unfortunately, John Innes compost varies in quality considerably from one manufacturer to the next. So to be sure of getting a consistent product look for the John Innes Manufacturers' Association Seal of Approval badge on the bag.

Pros

1 Provides a bottom-heavy stable base.
2 It's easy to keep watered.
3 Has a reserve of nutrients.
4 Loam from the garden is free.

Cons

1 Compaction can occur.
2 Poor drainage.
3 Needs sterilizing.
4 Heavy and dirty to handle.

Loam

A good friable garden soil from a well-cultivated vegetable plot would do, or for best results stack turves upside down and leave to rot. All loam should always be sieved and sterilized before use otherwise you'll risk being overrun with weeds.

Peat

Use a bale of ordinary horticultural grade moss or sedge peat – not too fine or too coarse. It should be slightly moist. Well-rotted leaf mould is an acceptable substitute.

Sand

Use a gritty sharp sand that has angular corners – made from graded crushed rock. Don't be tempted to use yellow builders' sand or any other that has been produced naturally by the forces of erosion. These sands have more rounded corners and so they compact together reducing aeration as well as the ability to drain.

Fertilizers

These are all widely available from garden centres and horticultural supply shops.

John Innes recipes are based on good garden loam which in time has become increasingly difficult to obtain and, of course, more expensive. This has resulted in further research that has led to the development of a new range of composts based not on loam but on peat.

Peat-based Composts

By far the most common type of composts sold nowadays are peat based composts. They can be split into three basic types: sowing, potting and general purpose. These vary mainly in their level of nutrients with sowing compost having the least, potting compost having the most and general purpose being a compromise between the two.

Pros

1 Good aeration.
2 Good water retention.
3 Free from pests and diseases.
4 Light to handle.
5 Clean.

Cons

1 Leaching can be a problem.
2 Top-heavy subjects tend to topple.
3 Need careful watering and feeding.

Peat

This medium provides the necessary water retention and aeration in the compost. It is a variable commodity available from many locations up and down the country, and so is usually blended to give a consistent product. Choose a graded moss or sedge peat available in bales.

Sand

Sand gives the compost weight and is now thought to help the re-wetting of compost once it has dried out. Use only angular horticultural grade sand.

Lime

Lime is essential to counter the inherent acidity of many peats. Too much acidity will cause nutrients to be 'locked up' and unavailable to plants.

Fertilizers

Any medium devoid of natural nutrients must have nitrogen, phosphorous and potash. However, it is also important to add trace elements like iron, manganese, zinc, boron and molybdenum which are needed by plants in minute quantities.

Specialist Composts

A range of specialist composts have been developed for those plants that don't grow well

Fig 25 Small heaters are ideal for the amateur greenhouse.

Making Your Own Compost

If you feel you would like to mix your own compost, here are the basic recipes.
Remember, a bushel is a dry measure of 8 gallons (36 litres) or four 2 gallon (9 litre) bucketfuls.

Basic Ingredients of Potting Compost

7 parts sterilized loam
3 parts peat
2 parts sharp sand

John Innes Potting Compost No. 1

To each bushel of basic ingredients add:

¾oz (21g) ground limestone or chalk
4oz (113g) John Innes base fertilizer

John Innes Potting Compost No. 2

To each bushel of basic ingredients add:

1½oz (42g) ground limestone or chalk
8oz (227g) John Innes base fertilizer

John Innes Potting Compost No. 3

To each bushel of basic ingredients add:

2¼oz (63g) ground limestone or chalk
12oz (336g) John Innes base fertilizer

John Innes Seed Compost

2 parts sterilized loam
1 part peat
1 part sharp sand

To each bushel add:
1½oz (42g) superphosphate
¾oz (21g) ground limestone or chalk

John Innes base fertilizer is available ready-made from most horticultural retailers or it can be made from the following recipe:

2 parts hoof and horn
2 parts superphosphate
1 part sulphate of potash

Making Your Own Peat-based Compost

Seed Compost

1 part peat
1 part sharp sand

To each bushel of ingredients add:

½oz (14g) sulphate of ammonia
1oz (28g) superphosphate
½oz (14g) sulphate of potash
4oz (113g) ground limestone or chalk

Potting Compost

3 parts peat
1 part sharp sand

To each bushel of ingredients add:

½oz (14g) sulphate of ammonia
½oz (14g) urea-formaldehyde (38 per cent nitrogen)
2oz (56g) superphosphate
1oz (28g) sulphate of potash
4oz (113g) ground limestone or chalk
2oz (56g) dolomite limestone
plus fritted trace elements

in the basic mediums. Ericaceous, alpine, orchid and cactus are just a few of those available.

Ericaceous is the most important of these and caters for those plants, like rhododendrons, azaleas, and many heathers, that prefer an acidic growing medium.

CONTAINERS

Like composts, containers have been revolutionized in recent years. Traditionally, clay pots and wooden seedtrays were used, but with the advent of cheaper cleaner plastic these stalwart materials have all but disappeared.

Pots

It is a shame that clay pots are an expensive rarity nowadays, since they offer a significant advantage over their plastic rival. It really all comes down to the clay's porous nature – allowing much needed air in to the compost and encouraging a more humid atmosphere around the pot by allowing water to escape in the form of vapour. This produces a healthier growing environment. Cheap pots have now taken over. They are easy to handle and clean, which is a great advantage during the busy spring period. In addition, plastic pots take up very little storage space. The following are a few of the advantages each has to offer.

Plastic

1 Cheap.
2 Easy to clean.
3 Wide range of styles available.
4 Light and easy to store.
5 Some designs almost unbreakable.

Clay

1 Porous.
2 Looks good and blends in.
3 Provides stability.
4 Good growing environment.

Fig 26 A small greenhouse can produce an abundance of colour, as shown with these fuchsias.

Seedtrays

Old-fashioned wooden seedtrays were heavy, took a lot of valuable storage space and were almost impossible to sterilize effectively. The plastic alternative doesn't suffer from any of these drawbacks, although they rarely survive more than a couple of seasons in my garden.

Furthermore, recent designs compartmentalizing the seedtray into modules are a real boon when you are trying to get your seedlings off to the best possible start by not disturbing the roots when potting on. The only previous alternative was to put each one in its own pot – and who has the space for that?

CHAPTER 5

Propagation

Few things are more satisfying to a gardener than the propagation of plants. To see something grow from a simple seed or cutting and develop, with tender loving care, to fruitful maturity, gives a real sense of achievement. Although all this can be done without a greenhouse, indeed without a garden at all, the range of plants you can propagate will be severely curtailed if you don't have the right growing environment. Furthermore, once you have caught the propagation fever you'll want to try your hand at everything.

SEED

How to Sow Seed

1. Select a container that has plenty of drainage holes and one that is not too deep – the more compost you use the more expensive the operation.
2. Fill your seedtray with seed compost (either loam-based or peat-based) and spread it out evenly with your finger tips to ensure there are no air holes.
3. Firm the compost lightly with a flat presser – either home-made from wood or a shop-bought version. If you're sowing in pots use the base of another pot to firm with.
4. Water the compost thoroughly using a fine-rosed watering can. Make sure the rose is pointing upwards so the water cascades gently onto the compost without disturbing the surface. Check that the rose doesn't dribble and rut the compost.
5. Leave the watered seedtrays for fifteen minutes or so, to drain excess water.

Fig 27 Firm the compost lightly with a flat presser.

Fig 28 Sow seed thinly and evenly over the surface of the compost.

30

6.   Sow the seed thinly and evenly over the surface of the compost. To achieve this fold one edge of the seed packet to form a V-shape, then hold the packet level in one hand and tap it gently with the forefinger of the other. Alternatively, pour the contents of the seed packet into one palm, cupping it a few inches above the prepared seedtray. Then tap it gently with the other hand. Both these methods should allow a continuous stream of seeds dropping singly onto the compost.

For very fine seed, such as begonia, lobelia, petunia, calceolaria and gloxinia, introduce some fine, dry silver sand into the seed packet. Mixed thoroughly with the seed, it acts as a spreading agent when the seed is sown in the normal way.
    Large seeds can be sown individually into pots of seed compost. Make a hole with a pencil or small dibber, place one seed in each hole and then top up the hole with compost.
    Cover surface-sown seeds with a layer of seed compost to prevent them drying out. To get an even coverage use a sieve. The depth of compost cover required will depend entirely on the type of seed you're sowing, so check the seed packet for directions. However, if you have collected your own seed or if the packet has been mislaid then a rough guide is to cover the seed with a depth of compost equal to the width of the seed. Dust-fine seed should not be covered at all.

Sowing Aftercare

1.   Label the seedtray carefully.
2.   Cover the tray with a clean sheet of glass and then a newspaper. This will keep warmth and humidity in and light, mice and next door's cat out.
3.   Place in a warm position, out of direct sunlight – usually 18–21°C. Check the directions on the seed packet or in the seed company's catalogue.
4.   Check the seedtrays every day if possible – remove the newspaper and glass as soon as seedlings emerge. Then move the seedtray to a

Fig 29   Label carefully and place in a plastic bag to reduce moisture loss.

light position out of direct sunlight so that the seedlings don't become drawn and spindly.
    The first leaves to appear are the so-called seed leaves. These nurture the seedling through its first few days until it produces its first true leaves.
5.   When the seedlings are large enough to handle, prick them out into another seedtray or individually into pots filled with potting compost, so they have room to develop. Handle young seedlings with great care; hold them by one seed leaf only, loosening the soil around the roots and support them as they are transferred. Never hold seedlings by their stems.
6.   Water in thoroughly and replace into a light position out of direct sunlight.

VEGETATIVE PROPAGATION

When viable seed is not available for one reason or another, or when plants don't grow true to type from the seed they produce, then they have to be propagated by vegetative means. Basically this method consists of taking a part of one individual and encouraging that part to produce a self-supporting root system and become an individual in its own right. Several methods are used in the greenhouse, including stem cuttings, leaf cuttings, layering and division.

31

Fig 30   Trim the cutting back to just below a leaf joint.

Fig 31   Remove lower leaves and dip the cut end in hormone rooting powder.

Softwood Cuttings

Fig 32   Insert cuttings around the edge of a pot using a small dibber.

Softwood cuttings are so-called because they are taken from current year's growth in spring and summer that has not had time to ripen and produce a woody outer layer. A wide range of plants, including pelargoniums, dahlias, chrysanthemums and fuchsias, can be increased in this way.

1.   Select healthy, strong, non-flowering shoots of current year's growth. Cut the shoots cleanly from the plant just above a leaf joint (node) using a sharp knife.
2.   At the work bench, trim up the cuttings, making your cut just below a node so that the final cutting is around 3in (7.5cm) long.
3.   Trim off the lower leaves close to the stem and remove any immature flowerbuds.
4.   Dip the cut end of each cutting into a little hormone rooting powder or liquid and tap it lightly to remove excess.
5.   Fill a container with compost and firm, lightly covering the surface with a little silver sand to aid drainage around each cutting.

6. Make a hole in the prepared compost using a small dibber and insert the cuttings to about half their length.

7. Firm and water.

Semi-ripe Cuttings

When shoots have developed a woody layer at their base in mid to late summer, they are said to be semi-ripe. Many garden trees and shrubs can be propagated using this method.

1. Select healthy sideshoots of the current year's growth between 4 and 5in (10 and 12.5cm) long. Tear the sideshoot from the branch by bending it backwards towards the main stem of the parent plant. This will produce a short snag of woody material (known as a heel) from the parent that needs to be trimmed up using a sharp knife.

2. Longer sideshoots should be cut from the parent plant cleanly, then trimmed back to about 4in (10cm).

3. Remove the lower leaves and reduce the leaf area of large-leaved plants by cutting each leaf back by half.

4. Dip the bottom of each cutting in hormone rooting powder, specially prepared for semi-ripe cuttings and shake off excess.

5. Insert prepared cuttings around the edge of a container filled with compost and dusted with silver sand.

6. Firm and water.

Leaf Cuttings

There are several types of leaf cuttings. Which method you use will depend on the plant being propagated. Saintpaulias, for instance, are increased by taking leaf and stalk cuttings.

How to take Saintpaulia Leaf Cuttings

1. Select a healthy, strong leaf that has developed fully but is not too old. Cut it cleanly

Fig 33 Tear the sideshoots from the branch, producing a short snag of woody material called a heel.

Fig 34 Trim up heel, dip in hormone rooting powder before inserting around the edge of a pot.

from its parent using a sharp knife, making sure no shimp is left that could rot back.

2. Trim up the leaf stalk to about 1in (2.5cm) long, then insert it into a pot of moist compost so that the stalk is about half buried.

3. Firm well.

4. Water Saintpaulia cuttings carefully making sure that no water gets onto the hairy leaves because they have a tendency to rot.

5. Soon roots will form and new plantlets will appear at the base of the old leaf stalks. When these plantlets are large enough to handle, they should be potted up singly. The old leaf stalk should be discarded.

How to take Streptocarpus Leaf Blade Cuttings

1. Choose a healthy, fully developed leaf and trim it from the parent.

2. Cut the leaf into sections: either in two longitudinally (removing the midrib), or laterally into several 1in (2.5cm) sections.

3. Dust hormone rooting powder over the cut ends to be inserted into the compost.

4. Place longitudinal cuttings into shallow slits made in the surface of the compost so that they stick up like sharks fins.

5. Insert lateral sections leaving two-thirds of each standing proud of the compost.

6. Plantlets develop around the cut ends of veins, but can take some time to appear. Keep compost moist and mist cuttings to prevent them drying out.

When large enough, carefully separate the new plantlets and pot up individually.

How to take Begonia Rex Whole Leaf Cuttings

1. Select a young, healthy leaf that is fully developed and remove it cleanly at the point it joins the parent plant.

2. Remove the stalk, then lay it on a flat surface before making several short cuts across the main veins – each about ½in (1.25cm) long and about

Fig 35 All that is needed for a whole leaf cutting.

Fig 36 Begonia rex *whole leaf cuttings. Make ½in (1.25cm) cuts across veins using a sharp knife.*

Fig 37 *Lay the leaf on moist compost and weigh it down with small stones.*

an inch or so apart. Dust each with hormone rooting powder.

3. Lay the leaf flat on the surface of moist cuttings compost, pressing it gently with your palm to get the cuts in good contact with the compost. Scatter a few small stones or something equally weighty to keep the leaf flat, or peg it down with bent pins.

4. Careful watering is important to prevent the rather exposed leaf from shrivelling.

5. Plantlets will form in a few weeks if all is well and these should be potted on singly into 3½in (9cm) pots using a potting compost.

Air Layering

Air layering is not a way of multiplying your stock quickly like the other methods already discussed. It is a technique you can turn to when your aralia or rubber plant gets a little too big or when it has dropped all its leaves and the bare stem is beginning to look unsightly.

1. Using a sharp, sturdy knife make a 2in (5cm)

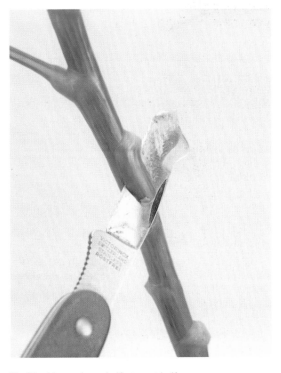

Fig 38 *Use a sharp knife to cut halfway through the stem.*

35

Fig 39 Dust cut surface with hormone rooting powder, then pack moss in the cut.

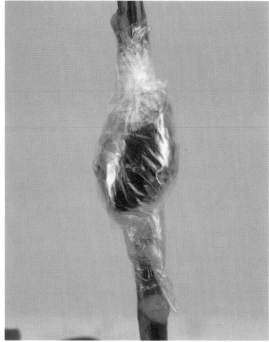

Fig 40 Put more moss around the cut to form a ball before wrapping in polythene.

upward incision a few inches below the last leaf so that the cut runs at an angle halfway through the stem. Support the stem with a cane.

2. Place a matchstick in the cut to hold it open while it is dusted with hormone rooting powder.

3. Remove the matchstick and replace with a handful of sphagnum moss.

4. Pack moss around the cut, forming a ball of moss around the stem. Then cover in polythene.

5. Seal the polythene at both ends, using adhesive tape.

6. When a good growth of roots can be seen in the ball of moss, the main stem of the parent plant can be cut through just below the roots and the resulting rooted top half of the plant potted up.

Division

Many multi-stemmed or clump-forming plants like ferns, orchids, agapanthus and aspidistra can be multiplied using this method. When in need of repotting in spring a pot-bound plant can be split into two or more sections, depending on its size – each with at least one plump bud and its own portion of the root system.

1. Water the plant to be divided, then leave it to drain for twenty-four hours.

2. Remove pot and any drainage crocks, then tease the roots apart, removing the compost as you go.

3. If the clump cannot be pulled apart by hand or where there's a crown, use a sharp knife to separate sections.

4. Dust larger cut surfaces with a powdered fungicide such as 'flowers of sulphur'. Then repot individually making sure the growing point remains just showing at the surface after firming. With very old plants the original central section may have to be discarded.

CHAPTER 6

The Greenhouse Year

JANUARY

January is usually the coldest month of the year and this can curtail gardening activities unless there is a greenhouse to hand. A heated greenhouse should be an inspiration of colour with primulas, calceolarias, cinerarias and cyclamen all brightening up an otherwise dull garden. Those with enough space for an Indian azalea or arum lily will be in for a treat this month.

Greenhouse Briefing

Careful heating, watering and ventilation is essential.

Flowers

Sow pelargoniums, salvia, gloxinia, hollyhocks and snapdragons.
Sow sweet peas for showing.
Take carnation and chrysanthemum cuttings.
Plant amaryllis, fibrous-rooted begonias and gloxinia tubers.
Pot up rooted cuttings.
Prune overwintered fuchsias and some greenhouse climbers.
Feed budding calceolarias, cinerarias and primulas.

Vegetables

Sow early tomatoes for heated greenhouses, dwarf French beans, leeks and onions.
Chit seed potatoes
Plant early pot-grown potatoes and rhubarb for forcing.

Fruit

Start early vines in heated greenhouses.

General Management

A careful balance must be maintained between heating, watering and ventilation during the tricky first few months of the year. Watering must be carried out with meticulous care, making certain the foliage and more particularly, the crown are not soaked. This will cause rot to set in and the dramatic collapse of foliage. It is best, therefore, to water from below during the early part of the day – soaking each plant thoroughly, then not returning to water again until the compost is quite dry. Do not overwater.

Incidentally, where a cyclamen plant does collapse it is worth checking the corm and root system for vine weevil larvae, which eat the fleshy roots. Where vine weevils are discovered throw out the affected plant and water others with a solution of gamma HCH.

Skilful ventilation is the secret to keeping fuel bills down. During bright, sunny, windless days open the ridge vents to allow a little air circulation within the greenhouse. On breezy days open the ridge vent on the leeward side of the greenhouse. Don't ventilate during very windy weather. When the vents are open it is worth shutting them a couple of hours before dusk to capture some of the sun's energy and give the heaters a head start.

All heaters and automatic ventilators should be checked regularly at this time of year. Paraffin heaters, in particular, need regular maintenance and filling, but don't be tempted to neglect the less demanding heating systems since any type can fail if not given proper care.

Maximum/minimum thermometers are an essential aid to the greenhouse grower, giving an accurate assessment of the temperature of the previous night. Use this information to adjust your heating and ventilation balance.

General maintenance of the greenhouse should not be neglected either; replace cracked or broken panes of glass promptly and examine the house looking for, and plugging, draughts. Check insulation for gaps or sagging – particularly in the roof sections – and fixing where necessary.

Check all overwintered stock of cuttings taken during the autumn. Remove and compost any yellowing leaves. Watch out for botrytis, grey mould fungus, because this can play havoc in the greenhouse at this time of year. Also peruse all your flowering plants on a regular basis, removing dead flowers promptly.

Daffodils, tulips and hyacinths can be brought inside from the plunge beds (sited in a sheltered spot in the garden) to maintain the continuity of flowering plants in the greenhouse. Don't send them into shock, though, by making this transfer too rapid; it is best to put them in a cold frame for a couple of days first.

Many house plants will now be suffering from the low light levels that occur indoors at this time of year. So it is worth bringing the worst affected into the greenhouse on a rota basis to keep them happy.

Cold greenhouses that are standing empty can be given the full clean-up treatment – scrubbing down the greenhouse structure and sterilizing soil and compost. (*See also* November, page 110). Any recently vacated or forgotten pots and seedtrays should be cleaned and stored in readiness for the busy sowing season ahead.

Flowers

Propagation

Sowing starts off at a gentle pace in January with half a dozen or so different plants to cope with. Many will germinate admirably with a temperature around 1–20°C – most economically provided by a propagator – although pelargonium, salvia and gloxinia prefer a couple of degrees more warmth.

Early sowings are particularly prone to attacks by fungus diseases. It is, therefore, worth making these sowings thinner than normal to allow better air circulation between the seedlings. Also water with a fungicide such as 'Cheshunt Compound' to give protection. Don't be tempted to go overboard with these early sowings because they will have to remain in the greenhouse until mid-May when space is always at a premium.

Sweet peas destined for the local flower show can be sown this month with heat. Nick the hard seed coat, or soak seed in warm water for twenty-four hours before sowing to speed germination. Sow three or four seeds about ½in (1.25cm) deep in 3½in (9cm) pots. Water thoroughly and maintain a temperature of around 16°C. For best results, though lay blotting or tissue paper in a shallow dish and soak with water. Lay the seed on the paper, then cover with another sheet of wet paper. The seeds will soon swell and produce a radicle within three or four days. Place germinated seed individually into special peat pot tubes for sweet peas about ½in (1.25cm) deep in a peat-based potting compost (or J.I.P No 2). Protect against mice feasting on the seed by covering sown pots with a sheet of glass.

Ordered seeds will soon be arriving from the seedhouses. They must be stored in a dry, frost-free place to keep them in top condition.

Cuttings of both carnations and chrysanthemums can be taken this month. Decorative varieties cut back to within 6in (15cm) last month and overwintered in the greenhouse will be producing fresh young shoots now. Select basal

SOWING IDEAS

Name	Germ. Temp.	Germ. Time	Plant Out	Comments
Althaea rosea (hollyhock)	13–15°C	1–3 weeks	April/May	Large pink flowers from July to September on rigid stems. Light green hairy leaves.
Antirrhinum majus (snapdragon)	16–18°C	1–3 weeks	March/June	Flowers from July to September in a variety of colours. Look for rust-resistant varieties.
Calceolaria Fl 'Anytime' Series	18–21°C	2–3 weeks	Pot grown	As the name suggests can be sown anytime for a show four months later.
Canna 'Seven Dwarfs' (Indian shot)	21–24°C	3–8 weeks	May	Ideal for bedding and indoors. Colours include scarlet, pink, orange, salmon and yellow. Bloom July to September.
Lathyrus odoratus (sweet pea)	13–18°C	1–3 weeks	April/May	Scented flowers in pink, white and purple are produced from June to September.
Lobelia erinus compacta	16–18°C	2–3 weeks	April/May	Many varieties with flowers varying in shades of blue set off against dainty foliage. Blooms May to September.
Pelargonium (geranium)	21–24°C	1–3 weeks	May	Continuous display from June to September of striking pinks, powerful reds and subtle whites.
Salvia patens	18–21°C	2 weeks	May	Provides a display of azure blue claw-shaped flowers on 2in (5cm) spikes in August and September.
Salvia splendens	18–21°C	2 weeks	May	Best known as summer bedding with its blazing red spike from July to September.
Sinningia speciosa (gloxinia)	21–24°C	2–4 weeks	Pot grown	Wider range of spectacular colours from May to August.
Verbena x hybrida	18–21°C	3–4 weeks	May	Many varieties available giving a wide range of sparkling colours from June to September.

Fig 41 Remove 3in (7.5cm) long basal shoots from the chrysanthemum stools using a sharp knife.

shoots around 3in (7.5cm) long that are not too drawn. Some varieties are a little slow in producing basal shoots so encourage them by adding a few handfuls of fresh compost around the stool and increasing the temperature a little. Do not cut shoots off right back to the stool but leave a ½in (1.25cm) stump, so that further shoots soon develop from the growth left behind. Use a sharp knife to trim up the cutting just below a leaf joint and remove the lower leaves. Dip in hormone rooting powder. Insert prepared cuttings either singly in the cells of a modular seedtray or two per 3½in (9cm) pot filled with a gritty cuttings compost with a layer of silver sand on top to aid drainage. Where many cuttings are being taken push them 2in (5cm) apart in boxes filled with compost. Water well.

Cuttings will not require watering again but it is worth spraying the tops with water to prevent them flagging too much. Although heat is not required, best results are obtained if the cuttings are placed in a propagator and given a little bottom heat. Rooting should occur within two or three weeks.

Charm chrysanthemums that have finished flowering need to be cut back. Keep them just moist in a frost-free position under the staging in the greenhouse or in a spare bedroom. Shoots will break from the stools during the next few weeks and make ideal material for cutting if you wish to increase your stock for display next year.

Perpetual-flowering carnations will produce sideshoots from nodes right up the stem. Avoid shoots close to the top of the plant as well as those around the base. As with the decorative chrysanthemums take 3in (7.5cm) cuttings – snapped cleanly out from the leaf joint on the parent plant. Using a sharp knife trim up the base, dip it in hormone powder and shake off excess. Push cuttings into a modular seedtray filled with cuttings compost or around the edge of a 3½in (9cm) pot. Water well. Place in a propagator and give a little bottom heat, 16°C if possible. Rooting will take place within a few weeks provided the tops are prevented from wilting. Both chrysanthemum and perpetual-flowering carnation cuttings would benefit from being rooted in a mist unit.

Standard fuchsias that have filled their 5in (12.5cm) pot and grown beyond the supporting split cane will be ready for moving into an 8in (20cm) pot. Replace the split cane with a 4ft

Fig 42 Kalanchoë.

(1.2m) long bamboo and pinch back sideshoots to the first pair of leaves. Where sideshoots are long enough they can be used as cutting material.

Trim each cutting just below a node using a sharp knife and remove lower leaves. Dip the cut end in hormone rooting powder and insert into a gritty cuttings compost. Maintain a temperature of around 16°C for speedy rooting.

Fuchsias grown as bushes will also need pinching out a week or so after potting up from their 3½in (9cm) pots into 5in (12.5cm) containers.

Planting

Hippeastrums that flowered last year can be brought into growth now. Every two or three years they will need re-potting. Using a peat-based compost (or J.I.P. No 2) in a 6in (15cm) pot, plant one bulb so that it is about two-thirds buried. In subsequent years just remove the top layer of compost and replace it with fresh. Aim for a temperature around 15°C and the bulb will soon produce the flat green tips of the leaves, quickly followed (and sometimes preceded) by a plump flowerbud. Water and feed as soon as growth is apparent. After the glorious blooms have gone over continue to feed and water the leaves until they turn yellow in late summer. Reduce watering, later leaving it off altogether, allowing the pot to dry out and the bulb to go into its annual dormant state over winter. Keep frost free. Repot, if necessary, the following spring for the process to be repeated.

Gloxinia tubers can also be started off by the end of January if you can maintain a temperature of around 21°C. Place tubers in a tray or box filled with moist peat to encourage the swelling buds into growth. Then pot each tuber up singly into 6in (15cm) pots filled with potting compost such as John Innes potting compost No. 2. It is probably better to choose loam-based compost because the plants get top heavy.

Once potted, grow plants in a lightly shaded position in a temperature of about 18°C. Keep well watered and feed once a fortnight.

Potting

Chrysanthemum and carnation cuttings taken last month or right at the beginning of this month, should have rooted and will need potting up individually into 3½in (9cm) pots filled with a peat-based compost (or J.I.P. No. 1).

Cyclamen seedlings sown in autumn can also be potted up.

Pruning

Overwintered fuchsias should be pruned back to produce a well-structured framework. Make each cut to an outward-facing bud ½in (1.25cm) or so from the main stem for standard types and to within 2in (5cm) of the crown for bush varieties.

Some greenhouse climbers such as the passion flower (*Passiflora*) need to be cut back if they're

Fig 43 Cut back overwintered fuchsias.

41

not to look straggly all season. Remove all weak and diseased shoots and prune back the current year's growth to a healthy, plump bud about 6in (15cm) from the main stem. Where the plant is becoming too big for the space available thin some shoots back to the main stem or even to ground level and cut others back as already described.

Feeding

Pot plants like calceolarias, cinerarias and primulas can be fed, with a high potash fertilizer to encourage flowerbud production.

Vegetables

Propagation

A range of early vegetables can be sown this month, the most important of which is the early tomato. You will need either plenty of room or not intend growing much else if you embark on cultivating early tomatoes in a heated greenhouse for first harvest in late June. Tomatoes need consistent heat, so a reliable well-regulated heating system is necessary to give a minimum temperature of 18°C from seedling stage until established. Temperatures can then be reduced gradually to 13°C at night until plants are ready for planting out, when a minimum of 10°C should be aimed for. If your heating system is not capable of maintaining such high temperatures early on or is not 100 per cent reliable then it would be wise to delay sowing until March, or buy in plants in April. Producing early tomatoes is an expensive gamble.

Sow very thinly. Tomato seed is large enough to sow singly so space six rows of four across a standard seedtray. Cover the seed with ¼in (6mm) of compost, water thoroughly, then place a sheet of glass and a newspaper over the seedtray. Maintain a temperature of 21°C for quick germination, but anywhere between 15 and 30°C would do.

Check the seedtray each day and wipe con-

Fig 44   Sow tomato seed individually spaced in a standard seedtray.

densation off the glass to prevent drips falling onto the compost and emerging seedlings. Remove the glass and newspaper as soon as the first seedlings break through, then put the seedtray in a light position to prevent the seedlings from becoming drawn. Keep out of direct sunlight.

When the first true leaves are expanding, lift the seedlings carefully and pot up individually into 3½in (9cm) pots. Do not handle them by their stems but hold one seedleaf between finger and thumb while supporting the root system with a small dibber or plant label. Discard any odd looking or small seedlings since they invariably both develop and fruit poorly.

The earliest crops of dwarf French beans can also be sown now and can be grown in the greenhouse borders before maincrop tomatoes put them in the shade. Varieties like 'Masterpiece' and 'The Prince' are often recommended. Sow 1in (2.5cm) deep during the latter half of January in peat pots in a temperature of 16°C. Water well. Plant out in the greenhouse border 6in (15cm) apart when roots start to show through the pot. Alternatively, sow five seeds in a 6in (15cm) pot filled with a peat-based potting compost (or J.I.P. No. 2).

Large onions and leeks for showing can be obtained if they are sown during January, in heat under glass, ready to be planted out as sturdy seedlings as the weather improves in late spring. Maintain a temperature of 16°C for best results, with seed sown individually in the cells of a modular seedtray or thinly in a standard seedtray filled with sowing compost.

To maintain a continuity of firm, crisp heads of lettuce in spring, sow the variety 'Marmer' direct into the greenhouse border. From sowing to harvesting takes just three or four months in a heated greenhouse and up to five months in an unheated one.

Bright scarlet radishes like the variety 'Robino' can be sown in succession from October to January in an unheated greenhouse to provide a much welcomed supply of fresh salad in early spring.

Planting and Forcing

Seed potatoes become available in January. Select healthy medium-sized tubers and set them in trays with the plumpest eyes uppermost. Keep in a frost-free position (under staging is ideal) — where they'll begin to sprout (chit). Also keep them out of reach of mice.

It is possible to plant a few tubers of early varieties such as 'Maris Bard' and 'Suttons Foremost' into large pots where they'll grow and produce a plateful of succulent early potatoes in late April and early May. A large pot or tub is required (12in (30cm) diameter) for forcing early potatoes. Cover the base with a 2in (5cm) layer of compost, then arrange three healthy, chitted tubers on the surface and cover these with a further 2in (5cm) of compost. Water well and keep in a light place maintaining a temperature of 10°C. As the fresh green shoots appear, topdress the pot with further compost to leave a couple of inches of shoot standing proud of the compost's surface. Repeat until the pot is full.

Fig 45 *Rebutia Muscula.*

Rhubarb crowns can be selected for forcing under greenhouse staging if not already done. Plunge them close together in a crate filled with moist peat, then cover with black polythene to encourage succulent pink shoots.

Fruit

You need a lot of space to grow fruit successfully in a greenhouse. Vines, peaches, nectarines, apricots and figs all benefit from a heated environment, but they are so demanding that little else can be grown with them.

A high temperature of 16°C is required if you want to start vines off at the end of January, with a minimum night temperature of around 7°C over the early spring period. A humid atmosphere must be maintained, which does not always fit in with other crops, and no ventilation should be given except on clear, still days. Feed and water well. Suitable varieties include 'Black Hamburg', 'Foster's Seedling' and 'Alicante'.

43

FEBRUARY

In most years February is a calm, dry and cold month. Greenhouse heaters are often working flat out day and night to maintain the required temperature, but still the heated greenhouse will reward us with a bounty of colour throughout the month. Again many primulas, calceolarias, cinerarias and cyclamen are in bloom. The vibrant calceolarias and stunning cinerarias provide an interesting contrast to the less showy primulas.

Greenhouse Briefing

Keep on top of greenhouse hygiene; wash and sterilize pots and seedtrays.
Continue careful heating, watering and ventilation.
Check insulation.

Flowers

Sow half-hardy annuals and perennials.
Sow sweet peas, bedding dahlias and several greenhouse pot plants.
Take cuttings from chrysanthemums and carnations.
Plant achimene tubers.
Prune greenhouse fuchsias, bougainvilleas, gardenia and overwintered pelargoniums.

Vegetables

Sow early melons and cucumbers for raising in a heated greenhouse.
Sow broad beans and early peas if not done in autumn.
Sow early lettuce, cauliflower, cabbage and Brussels sprouts.

Fruit

Hand pollinate early peaches, nectarines and apricots as well as early vines.
Bring potted strawberry runners inside.

General Management

Hygiene is important at this time of year when ventilation is limited and temperatures are down. Systematically purge the greenhouse of dead and dying leaves and promptly remove flowers that are past their prime. Check for pests and diseases now to prevent them getting an early foothold. Spray as necessary.

Ventilation is of paramount importance but once again, it should only occur during calm, sunny spells. Don't be tempted to open up the vents on dank, misty days or when there's a keen wind blowing that might cause a drop in temperature inside the greenhouse. Automatic vents can be a problem at this time of year because they tend to open too wide and remain ajar right into the evening, losing valuable heat right at the end of the day.

Watering must be given as and when necessary – a great deal more will be required by plants in active growth on bright sunny days. Most winter watering is best done from below by standing the pot plant in a tray and then adding water or immersing the pot up to its rim in a bowl of water for a few minutes. Whichever method is used, a pot plant must be given an opportunity to drain fully before being returned to its position on the staging.

The weather dictates most activities in the greenhouse and none more so than heating. The choice of cleaning, filling and trimming the wick of paraffin heaters makes them unpopular these days. In addition they have to be lit every time the temperature threatens to plummet. Other forms of heating need less maintenance and are often thermostatically controlled to make them more fuel efficient. But even these systems should be checked regularly just in case something goes wrong. After all, it only takes one penetrating frost to wipe out all your early spring efforts.

It is not worth heating the entire greenhouse just to get a few garden crops off to an early start. It is far better to invest in a soil-warming cable and install it in a partitioned-off section of

Fig 46   Opuntia Subulata.

the greenhouse. Soil-warming cables are cheap to run and provided there is already an electricity supply are easy to install (*see also* Greenhouse Equipment, page 15). The heat produced by soil-warming cables raises the temperature of the compost in pots and seedtrays placed on top – this speeds germination and encourages root development. If you intend getting one buy it now to realize maximum benefit from your investment.

Check through the stock of pots and seedtrays to make sure they are ready for use as well as ensuring there are sufficient labels for the coming season. Sit down and run through the sowing programme for the weeks ahead to check there will be continuity of supply through the season. Use rubber bands to group packets of seeds that can be sown at the same time under the same or very similar conditions. This highlights those requiring special treatment. Make a checklist for all these jobs otherwise something is bound to be forgotten.

The foliage remaining on bulbs forced for Christmas will now be looking a little tired. Don't trim up these leaves, though, but place the pots in a light position ready to be planted out in a sheltered spot in the garden as soon as the weather allows. It will take a couple of seasons before they recover from being forced. Once forced, bulbs cannot be induced to flower early a second year.

Check that insulation is already in place for gaps and draughts and tape up any you find. Sagging insulation should be given further support. Greenhouses not yet in use will need to be insulated for the next few months to save on fuel. A wide range of materials is available, including the cheap and versatile, but rather inefficient, polythene sheeting and the more expensive, but far more effective, bubble polythene that gives a double-glazing effect.

Flowers

Propagation

Sowing begins in earnest now, so get yourself organized. Make sure there is enough compost for the coming weeks.

Many half-hardy annuals can be sown this month which are destined to decorate beds and borders throughout the garden. Sow plenty; any extras are always useful for passing on to or swapping with friends and neighbours.

Sow sweet peas for the garden this month. Prepare seed by either nicking the hard seed coat with a knife or soaking the seed in warm water for twenty-four hours before sowing. Any seed that doesn't respond by swelling should be nicked to encourage water absorption. Sow three or four seeds in a 3½in (9cm) pot or individually in sweet pea tubes filled with sowing compost (or J.I.P. No. 2). Maintain a temperature of around 16°C for quick germination.

Bedding dahlias need to be sown during February or March in a seedtray at a temperature of 16°C. Germination will quickly occur and new seedlings should be potted up individually as soon as they can be handled safely. The dwarf Coltness hybrids such as 'Disco Mixed' and 'Redskin' are tried and trusted varieties.

Cuttings can still be taken from chrysanthemum which have been stools forced into growth earlier this year (see also January, page 40). Pot up rooted cuttings individually into 3½in (9cm) pots filled with a peat-based potting compost (or J.I.P. No. 1) to prevent them being checked by lack of nutrients in the cuttings compost. Take great care when teasing roots apart to prevent damage.

Similarly take further cuttings from carnations and pot up those that have rooted. Place all recently potted plants in a light, but cool spot out of direct sunlight.

Border dahlias can also be increased now. Select some healthy tubers that have been stored over winter in a cool, dark, frost-free place. These can now be boxed in a moist peat and sand mix with their crowns clear of the surface. Place in a warm, light position so the tubers swell and start to produce shoots suitable for making cuttings. You should aim for a temperature of around 16°C for a good supply of short-jointed, fresh green shoots. When new shoots are 3–4in (7.5–10cm) long, cut them off with a sharp knife, leaving a ½in (1.25cm) stump from which the new shoots will develop. Then treat as softwood cuttings (see also Propagation, page 32).

Planting

Pot up achimenes grub-like tubers to get an impressive display in several glorious colours. Six or eight tubers can easily be accommodated in a 6in (15cm) pot and will give a good display. Either plant about 1in (2.5cm) deep direct in the pot using a proprietary potting compost or lay the tubers on the surface and give them a slight covering of compost. Once sprouted they can be potted up. Whatever the method used, the tubers should be watered well and kept in a temperature of 16°C until signs of growth can be

Fig 47 Pot up achimenes grub-like tubers and cover with 1in (2.5cm) of compost.

clearly seen.

Subsequently the plants should be fed at fortnightly intervals. If you have enough tubers it is nice idea to stagger the starting dates of each potful to get an extended flowering display.

Pruning

Greenhouse fuchsias are best pruned back hard at the end of February to prevent straggly growth spoiling the plants appearance. Like bougainvilleas and gardenias that also need pruning now, each main shoot on the overwintered fuchsia needs to be cut back by a half or two-thirds and the laterals trimmed back to a plump, healthy bud.

Of course, all weak, tangled, diseased or dead growth must be completely removed. Pelargoniums, too, need a trim after their winter rest. Cut back to about 6in (15cm) and repot with fresh compost.

SOWING IDEAS

Name	Germ. Temp.	Germ. Time	Plant Out	Comments
Annuals:				
Alyssum maritimum	10–15°C	2 weeks	April	Mound-forming plants covered in blooms from June to September.
Celosia plumosa 'Century Mixed'	18–21°C	2 weeks	May/June	Good pot plants and bedding if hardened off carefully. Bloom all summer.
Felicia bergeriana (kingfisher daisy)	15–18°C	2 weeks	April/May	Mat-forming plant with grey hairy leaves. Flowers summer and autumn.
Gerbera jamesonii (Transvaal daisy)	15–18°C	2–3 weeks	May	Fabulous coloured large blooms on strong stems from May to August.
Latherus odoratus (sweet pea)	13–18°C	1–3 weeks	April/May	Scented flowers in pink, white and purple are produced from June to September.
Matthiola incana 'Mixed' (East Lothian stocks)	13–15°C	2 weeks	April/May	Flowers appear June and July on 12in (30cm) spikes in colours ranging from white to purple.
Nicotiana alata (tobacco plant)	18–21°C	2–3 weeks	May	Blooms from July to September producing a sweet scent. Grow in shade if you want to see flowers open during the day.
Perennials:				
Althea rosea (hollyhock)	13–15°C	1–3 weeks	May	Large single or double pink flowers from July to September on rigid stems.
Antirrhinum majus (snapdragon)	16–18°C	1–3 weeks	April/June	Flowers from July to September in a variety of colours. Look for rust-resistant varieties.
Calceolaria 'Anytime Series'	18–21°C	2–3 weeks	Pot grown	Sow at any time for a spectacular show just four months later. Many colours.

47

SOWING IDEAS

Name	Germ. Temp.	Germ. Time	Plant Out	Comments
Canna 'Seven Dwarfs' (Indian shot)	21–24°C	3–8 weeks	May	Ideal for summer bedding and in pots. Many colours from July to September.
Catananche caerulea (Cupid's dart)	13–15°C	2–3 weeks	May	Summer flowers of brilliant sky-blue. Good as cut flowers in water.
Chrysanthemum parthenium	13–15°C	2 weeks	April/May	Yellow and white varieties produced freely from July to September.
Lobelia erinus compacta	16–18°C	2–3 weeks	April/May	Blooms from May to September. Many varieties with flowers in varying shades of blue.
Pelargonium (geranium)	21–24°C	1–3 weeks	May	Much loved bedding and pot plant that produces its colours in pink, powerful reds and subtle whites.
Salvia patens	18–21°C	2 weeks	May	August to September produces azure blue claw-shaped flowers on a spike 2in (5cm) tall.
Salvia splendens	18–21°C	2 weeks	May	Produces its blazing red spike from July to September. Very popular bedding plant.
Sinnigia speciosa (gloxinia)	21–24°C	2 weeks	Pot grown	Range of spectacular colours produced from May to August.
Tropaeolum peregrinum (canary creeper)	13–16°C	2 weeks	April/May	Fast growing creeper that produces lots of pretty yellow flowers all summer.
Verbena × hybrida	18–21°C	3–4 weeks	May	Flowers June to September with the large number of varieties producing wide range of colours.

Fig 48   Exacum.

Vegetables

Propagation

Melon seed needs to be sown in succession from now until May if you want plants cropping all summer. Early sowings will need a well-heated greenhouse for the first few months. The easy to grow 'Gaylia' that produces sweet and aromatic fruit and the productive 'Ogen' with its delicate pale green flesh are two varieties worth considering. Sow two seeds in a 3½in (9cm) pot filled with compost. Place each flat seed on its edge to prevent rotting, about ½in (1.25cm) deep using a small dibber. Place pots in a tray and water. Allow the pots to drain, then lay a sheet of glass and a piece of paper over the top and maintain a temperature of at least 18°C but preferably 21°C. Check the pots each day and remove the glass and paper as soon as the first seedlings appear. The glass will also protect the seed from avaricious mice that find melon seeds irresistible.

Cucumbers for an early crop can also be sown now, provided there is a good heating system that is 100 per cent reliable. Unlike melons, only one sowing is necessary since the plants will, with luck, crop the entire season if given the correct treatment. Try an all-female variety such as 'Uniflora' which can yield for up to six months. Select 3½in (9cm) pots and sow two seeds per pot as for melons. Cucumbers require a germination temperature of around 24°C and can be emerging in just a week or so. Remove the weakest seedling from each pot.

If you were unable to sow broad beans last autumn then sow them now in pots in the greenhouse. Use 3½in (9cm) pots and sow the beans individually ¾in (2cm) deep in a peat-based seed compost. No heat is required – just frost-free nights. Even a well-insulated frame would do. Harden off next month for planting out in April.

Sow early pea varieties such as 'Little Marvel' and 'Early Onward' if the November sowing direct outside was missed. Sow in pots. A novel method is to sow in a compost-filled gutter pipe. Sow two rows 2–3in (5–7.5cm) apart with seed staggered down the pipe. A temperature of around 13°C will be sufficient.

The slow to germinate aubergine (egg plant) should be sown under glass during February. Sow singly into peat pots filled with sowing compost and maintain a temperature of at least 18°C.

First crops of outdoor lettuce can be sown in a temperature of 13°C. Varieties such as 'Fortune', 'Susan' and 'Unrivalled' should be sown ¼in (6mm) deep into peat blocks or fibre pots for best results. Once germinated, harden off in a cold frame and plant outside from mid-March onwards provided the weather is suitable. Alternatively, make further sowings of the 'Iceberg' type lettuce, 'Marmer', direct into the greenhouse border where the temperature is kept above freezing for harvesting in May.

If you have a heated greenhouse it's a good time to make first sowings of cauliflower; cabbage and Brussels sprout. Again a temperature of around 13°C or slightly above is ideal. Sow seed very thinly in a seedtray or individually in a modular seedtray using a sowing compost.

Start to harden off autumn-sown early-summer cauliflowers for planting out next month.

Growing Bags

The growing bag has changed the face of greenhouses during the summer months. It is simply a plastic sack filled with a mixture of peat, fertilizer and trace elements in sufficient quantities to promote balanced growth through the first couple of months. This enables even the most inexperienced gardener to get the plants off to a flying start. They give the greenhouse grower the chance to crop the greenhouse intensively year after year. In addition, because the growing medium is new each year it will almost eliminate the carry-over of many pests and diseases associated with growing in border soil.

The relatively small volume of compost does, however, make watering of critical importance – particularly with thirsty crops such as cucumbers, melons and tomatoes. In hot periods during the summer, frequent waterings are needed – at least once a day. If plants become stressed because of a lack of water then disorders like blossom-end rot in tomatoes can result.

Fruit

Pollination

During February peaches, nectarines and apricots in a well-heated greenhouse start to come into flower. They are normally insect pollinated but in the greenhouse this is a far from reliable method so some form of assistance must be given. Using a soft paintbrush, or something similar, transfer pollen from one flower to another by gently dabbing the brush into each flower. The most effective time is just around noon when the greenhouse is warmest. During this period the greenhouse needs to be kept constantly warm to get a good set. After setting, syringe the plants daily.

Vines also need hand pollinating when they come into flower – this month for those plants started into growth during January.

Unheated greenhouses with vines should be well ventilated during the day to prevent plants shooting away too early and risking frost damage to the soft, young growth.

Starting

Bring inside pot-grown strawberry runners that were rooted during late July and early August and pot into 5in (12.5cm) containers. These plants need to be started into growth very gradually, raising the temperature slowly to about 10°C at night. When new growth appears, increase water rations. Several varieties are recommended including 'Gorella', 'Grandee', 'Redgauntlet', 'Rival', 'Tamella' and 'Cambridge Vigour'.

MARCH

March, it is said, comes in like a lion and goes out like a lamb. True or not, it is often a stormy month with the odd week or so of fine weather. In the greenhouse the permanent staging provides the backbone of colour during this month with the beautiful and varied species of *Primula*, such as *malacoides, kewensis, obconica* and *sinensis*. Lovely colour combinations and delicate fragrance of recent introductions has lead to a revival of this underrated pot plant.

Greenhouse Briefing

Ventilate as required.
Check temperatures regularly.
Maintain heating equipment.

Flowers

Sow many annuals, biennials, perennials, cacti, fuchsias and geraniums.
Prick out seedlings as necessary.
Continue to take chrysanthemum, dahlia and fuchsia cuttings.
Divide border dahlia tubers.
Pot-on early carnations and chrysanthemum cuttings.
Harden off autumn-struck cuttings.
Plant tuberous begonias and cannas.

Vegetables

Successional sowings of salad vegetables.
Sow herbs, summer cabbage, cauliflowers and winter celery.

Sow melons, cucumbers, sweet peppers and aubergines as well as tomatoes for unheated greenhouses and outside.

General Management

Space will soon become a limiting factor in the greenhouse. It is, therefore, worth spending a little time at the beginning of March to erect extra temporary staging and shelving to double, treble or even quadruple the available growing space. Use the permanent staging, if any, for pot plants, and propagator. Keep any recently sown seedtrays underneath, but don't stack them up otherwise you will find it difficult to check for germination. As seeds germinate move them out into a light position, using the temporary staging and shelving.

The lengthening days and warmer, sunny spells will make maintaining a constant temperature in the greenhouse a challenge. A couple of hours of midday sun can send the temperatures soaring, yet an overcast day can be cold and dingy. Ventilation is the only means of controlling rises in temperature at this time of year, so an automatic vent is essential unless you intend spending all day, every day in the greenhouse.

Use a maximum/minimum thermometer to check the automatic vent is set correctly and also make sure the constant opening and closing hasn't upset the tight fitting of the vents when shut. Cold draughts can be very damaging to soft, young shoots.

Continue to check heaters on a regular basis right through this month. For the majority of greenhouse crops aim for a temperature of around 7°C at night and 16°C during the day. This rise should not be allowed to occur in one go but in several stages throughout the morning by careful ventilation, followed by a similarly gradual decrease during the afternoon.

Watering will be more frequent this month but far less critical. Water regularly, keeping a careful check on those seedlings with small root systems and plants in small volumes of compost – those in modular seedtrays, for instance. Time taken watering will be ever-increasing through the spring and summer, so perhaps it would be worth considering some form of automatic assistance. Capillary matting on the bench is an effective way of watering established pot plants and the drip or dribble automatic irrigation systems are ideal for watering growing bags or plants grown in the border soil (*see also* Greenhouse Equipment, page 22).

Keep an eye open for signs of damping off. Where this occurs remove affected seedlings and water others with a solution of 'Cheshunt Compound'. Hygiene is most important this month. If pests and diseases become established they'll plague your efforts all summer long. Take the necessary remedial action to combat invaders as soon as possible – delay will often mean repeat sprays and loss of crop vigour.

Fumigation is often worthwhile early on. Not only does it clear the greenhouse of unwanted visitors, but if the outside of the structure is inspected leaks can easily be seen. These then can be plugged up to prevent draughts and heat loss.

Flowers

Propagation

The pace of sowing is at its peak now so it is prudent to have a system worked out in advance to utilize the rapidly diminishing shelf and staging areas to best effect. A rotation system can be effective so that seedlings of different ages don't get mixed up and left to grow too big before pricking out or potting on.

Nearly anything sown last month can be sown this month, plus many cacti, fuchsias, geraniums and herbs as well as half-hardy annuals, greenhouse annuals, herbaceous perennials and many alpines.

Check seedlings regularly for germination – at least once a day. When the first shoots poke their heads clear of the compost surface, remove the seedtray from the relative darkness of lower staging to a position of good light but out of direct sun. Remove any glass and paper used to

Fig 49   Prick out seedlings as soon as they are large enough to handle.

cover the seedtray while seeds were germinating. As soon as seedlings are large enough to handle, carefully tease them free of the compost – keeping their small, but vital, root system intact – supporting each seedling from beneath using a dibber or pencil and steadying it by holding one seedleaf between finger and thumb. Never pick up a seedling by its fragile stem.

Depending on the size of the seedling as well as space available, transfer the seedlings either individually into pots or line them out in a seedtray.

Continue to take cuttings of both chrysanthemums and dahlias as suitable shoot growth becomes available. Don't make the mistake of taking ten times the number of cuttings from one variety simply because it readily produces that many more shoots, otherwise the eventual display will look rather unbalanced.

Border dahlia tubers not used to produce cuttings can be increased by division this month. Check that the tubers are healthy before placing them in boxes containing a moist peat and sand mix. Make sure their crowns are not buried. Keep in a cool, light place to encourage dormant buds to swell.

Fig 50   A small greenhouse is ideal for germinating seeds.

Fig 51 *Divide dahlia tubers, using a sharp knife.*

Fig 52 *Pinch out the growing tip of chrysanthemum plants to encourage several shoots to develop.*

Using a sharp knife, cut the crown into good-sized sections each with healthy tubers and a cluster of plump buds. Dust the cut sections with a fungicide such as 'flowers of sulphur' to prevent rotting. Plant out when conditions are suitable.

Softwood cuttings of several greenhouse plants such as fuchsias and pelargoniums can be taken now. The number taken will depend on how many losses were incurred during the long, freezing winter months. All new shoots can be used, but wait until the cuttings are at least 2in (5cm) (pelargoniums) and 1½in (3.75cm) (fuchsias).

Training

Fuchsias being trained as standards will need their sideshoots pinched out after the first pair of leaves. The leading shoot should be kept straight by using a bamboo cane and ties. Once at the required height, pinch the leading shoot out and allow the next six or seven sideshoots to develop to form the head.

Fuchsias can also be planted up in hanging baskets. If done now the plants will have plenty of time to settle in and may well be in flower when they go outside. Line the basket with moss and place an old saucer in its base to help retention of moisture. Fill the lined basket with potting compost and plant three or four fuchsias in a 12in (30cm) diameter basket. Once the plants are established, pinch out the growing tips to encourage bushiness.

Early carnations and chrysanthemum cuttings will have rooted and started putting on growth rapidly. When they reach about 4in (10cm) high and have put on six or seven leaves it is time to pinch them out. Take them back to about 3in (7.5cm), removing one or two leaf joints. Do this by holding the plant firmly between finger and thumb at the desired leaf joint, then move the growing tip sharply from one side to the other. The top will break out cleanly. This action encourages the development of basal sideshoots, producing a sturdier, bushy plant.

54

SOWING IDEAS

Name	Germ. Temp.	Germ. Time	Plant Out	Comments
Annuals:				
Ageratum houstonianum 'Blue Mink'	15–18°C	2 weeks	May/June	A rather compact plant that produces powder-blue flowers from early spring to the first frost.
Alyssum maritimum	10–15°C	2 weeks	April	Mound-forming plants covered in blooms from June to September.
Amaranthus caudatus (love-lies-bleeding)	15–18°C	2 weeks	May	Striking ropes of blood-red blooms sometimes reaching 2ft (60cm) long.
Arctotis grandis (African daisy)	15–18°C	3–4 weeks	April/May	Grey-blue centre surrounded by delicate white and pink petals – blooms during summer months.
Begonia semperflorens	18–21°C	2–4 weeks	May/June	Red, pink or white flowers are produced from June to September.
Brachycome iberidifolia 'Mixed' (Swan river daisy)	18–21°C	2 weeks	May	Pink, blue and white starry flowers are fragrant and appear from late June until the first frost of Autumn.
Callistephus chinensis (China aster)	15–18°C	2–4 weeks	May	Daisy-like flowers from July until October in shades of red, pink, yellow and purple.
Celosia argenta plumosa 'Century Mixed' (Prince of Wales feather)	18–21°C	2 weeks	May/June	Need to be hardened off carefully before planting out. Blooms all summer long.
Cleome spinosa	18–21°C	2 weeks	May	White blooms flushed with pink appear from July onwards. Several good coloured varieties.
Convolvulus tricolor 'Dwarf Rainbow Flash'	15–18°C	1–2 weeks	May	Intense blue flowers with starkly contrasting centres of yellow and white. Appear all summer.

SOWING IDEAS

Name	Germ. Temp.	Germ. Time	Plant Out	Comments
Annuals:				
Coreopsis tinctoria	15–18°C	2 weeks	May	Brilliant yellow, red and in between shades on stems. From July to September.
Didiscus caeruleus (blue lace flower)	15–18°C	1–2 weeks	May	Dainty soft powder-blue flowers in July and August. Ideal for bedding or as a summer pot plant.
Dimorphotheca aurantiaca (star of the Veldt)	15–21°C	1–2 weeks	May	Superb for tubs, windowboxes, baskets, walls and rockery. Blooms from June to September in various colours.
Felicia bergeriana (kingfisher daisy)	15–18°C	2 weeks	April/May	Mat-forming plant with grey hairy leaves. Flowers summer and autumn.
Gerbera jamesonii (Transvaal daisy)	15–18°C	2–3 weeks	May	Fabulous coloured large blooms on strong stems from May to August.
Gomphrena globosa 'Buddy' (bachelor's buttons)	15–21°C	1–2 weeks	May	Long-lasting blooms in deep purple appear from July to September. Ideal pot plant.
Helianthus annuus 'Sunburst Mixed' (sunflower)	15–18°C	2 weeks	May	Red, yellow, bronze and gold blooms, 4in (10cm) across on strong branching stems.
Hibiscus trionum 'Sunnyday' (flower-of-an-hour)	15–18°C	1–2 weeks	May	2in (5cm) blooms in pale yellow with a purple centre. Flowers all summer long.
Impatiens balsamina 'Double Mixed' (balsam)	18–21°C	3–4 weeks	May/June	Suitable for growing in pots under glass. Blooms in a range of colours produced from June to September.
Ipomoea purpurea	18–21°C	1–2 weeks	May/June	Richly coloured blooms 2in (5cm) across all summer.
Ipomoea tricolor 'Heavenly Blue' (morning glory)	18–21°C	1–2 weeks	May/June	Produces early blooms in stunning sky-blue.

SOWING IDEAS

Name	Germ. Temp.	Germ. Time	Plant Out	Comments
Annuals:				
Kochia scoparia trichophylla (burning bush)	15–21°C	1–2 weeks	May	Much underrated plant that produces a clean pale green mound of foliage that gradually turns deep red.
Lychnis coronaria alba	15–18°C	1–2 weeks	May	Superb plant for silver and white border. Grey hairy foliage and white flowers produced from July to September.
Matthiola bicornis (night scented stock)	13–15°C	2 weeks	April/May	Rather dull lilac blooms on spikes between July and August. At night they open to produce a heady scent.
Matthiola incana 'Mixed' (East Lothian stocks)	13–15°C	2 weeks	April/May	Flowers appear in June and July on 12in (30cm) spikes in a range of colours from white to purple.
Moluccella laevis (shellflower)	15–21°C	2–3 weeks	May	Spikes of white fragrant flowers each surrounded by a shell-like green calyx.
Nemesia strumosa 'Carnival Mixed'	15–18°C	2 weeks	May	Funnel-shaped blooms in a range of colours produced from June to August. Look best when planted close together in a group.
Nicotiana alata (tobacco plant)	18–21°C	2–3 weeks	May	Blooms from July to September producing a sweet scent. Grow in shade if you want to see flowers open during the day.
Phlox drummondii	13–15°C	2 weeks	May	From July to September blooms in varying shades from white to purple.
Reseda odorata (mignonette)	13–15°C	1–2 weeks	May	Small ¼in (6mm) blooms are produced all summer long in yellow or orange.

SOWING IDEAS

Name	Germ. Temp.	Germ. Time	Plant Out	Comments
Annuals:				
Tagetes erecta (African marigold)	15–18°C	1 week	May	Dark green leaves set off the scented yellow blooms produced from July until the first frost.
Tagetes patula (French Marigold)	15–18°C	1 week	May	Deep orange and yellow blooms 2in (5cm) aross. Produced all summer long.
Tagetes tenuifolia (marigold)	15–18°C	1 week	May	Yellow flowers 1in (2.5cm) across, produced from July to September.
Thunbergia alata (black-eyed Susan)	15–21°C	2–3 weeks	May/June	2in (5cm) wide flowers are produced from July onwards. Orange petals with purple central tube.
Zinnia elegans	18–21°C	2–3 weeks	May/June	Produces blooms from July to September in a range of colours from white to red.
Perennials:				
Alstroemeria ligtu (Peruvian lily)	18–21°C	4–5 weeks	Early summer	Pink and orange blooms in June and July. A half-hardy species that grows to about 24in (60cm).
Alyssum saxatile 'Golden Green'	10–15°C	2 weeks	May	Ground-hugging plant with grey foliage that is covered in masses of tiny yellow blooms in the spring.
Antirrhinum majus (snapdragon)	16–18°C	1–3 weeks	April/June	Flowers from July to September in a variety of colours.
Calceolaria Hyb. 'Anytime Series'	18–21°C	2–3 weeks	Pot grown	Sow any time for a show four months later. Various colours.
Canna 'Seven Dwarfs' (Indian shot)	21–24°C	3–8 weeks	May	Ideal for bedding and indoors. Colours include scarlet, pink, orange, salmon and yellow. Bloom from July to September.

SOWING IDEAS

Name	Germ. Temp.	Germ. Time	Plant Out	Comments
Perennials:				
Catananche caerulea (Cupid's dart)	13–15°C	2–3 weeks	May	Summer flowers of brilliant sky-blue.
Dianthus chinensis 'Fire Carpet' (Indian pink)	13–15°C	2–3 weeks	May	A perpetual unabated sea of vermilion scarlet from June until the first frost.
Heliotropium X hybrid 'Marine'	18–21°C	1–4 weeks	May	Large fragrant, purple flowers produced all summer. Deep green foliage. Can be used as bedding or in pots.
Mesembryanthemum criniflorum (Livingstone daisy)	15–18°C	2 weeks	May	Starry flowers in a variety of colours that are produced through the summer. Prefers a sunny spot.
Petunia X hybrida	15–18°C	2–3 weeks	May/June	Wide range of varieties that produce a fabulous display all summer. Select smallest seedlings because they produce the best colours.
Salvia patens	18–21°C	2 weeks	May	Provides an August and September display of azure blue claw-shaped flowers.
Salvia splendens	18–21°C	2 weeks	May	Best known as summer bedding with its easily recognizable blazing red flower spike. From July to September.
Sinningia speciosa (gloxinia)	21–24°C	2–4 weeks	Pot grown	Beautiful display from May to August with spectacular blooms in range of colours.
Tropaeolum peregrinum (canary creeper)	13–18°C	2 weeks	April/May	Fast growing creeper that produces lots of pretty yellow flowers all summer.
Verbena X hybrida	18–21°C	3–4 weeks	May	Many varieties available giving a wide range of sparkling colours from June to September.

Hardening Off

Frames now congested with cuttings taken during the autumn, as the newly rooted plants break into growth, should be opened during the day to slowly harden them off. Increase the cuttings' exposure a little each fine, calm day, but keep the frame closed on very cold or windy days as well as every night.

Planting

For a profusion of magnificent blooms in a rainbow of colours from May to November start tuberous begonias into growth now. Select only firm, healthy tubers and place them in trays filled with moist peat, hollow side facing upwards. If the temperature is kept around the 18°C mark then plump buds will soon swell ready for moving on either individually into 6in (15cm) pots or several planted into larger containers. Pendulous varieties like 'Pendula Chanson Mixed' and 'Basket Mixed' with their semi-double blossoms of copper, scarlet, crimson, white and yellow are ideal for planting in a hanging basket or tub to get a waterfall of colours.

Stunning cannas add an exotic touch to borders during the summer and can be started now in pots in the greenhouse. Plant fleshy root sections in 3½in (9cm) pots filled with a peat-

Fig 53   Pot Lily.

Fig 54 Chrysanthemum.

based potting compost. Water well and aim to maintain a temperature of about 15°C.

Vegetables

Propagation

Many crops that are required throughout the summer will need to be sown in small batches several times in succession through the spring. The belief that it is possible to sow only once, grow the most vigorous seedlings on quickly and get a succession by delaying pricking out and the potting of others is mistaken. Any plant given a poor start or checked by delays will never perform well later in the season. It is far better to plan out a succession of sowings every couple of weeks or so, pricking out and potting on when the seedlings are ready.

Radish and lettuce are a good example. Earliest sowings made this year continue on from those made at the end of last and should be repeated at fortnightly intervals through February and March. The most vigorous seedlings should then be selected to provide a succession of delicious early salad vegetables while they're so expensive in the shops. Sowings can be made now in unheated greenhouses or cold frames and by the end of the month they can be made direct under cloches outside.

61

Herbs are normally sown direct outside in late spring, but a few half-hardy species, such as bush basil (*Olinum minimum*) and sweet basil (*Olinum basilicum*), will benefit from a slightly earlier sowing under a warmer environment. Sow into a half seedtray or pan filled with seed compost. Prick out seedlings when large enough to handle safely into 3½in (9cm) pots filled with a peat-based potting compost. Thyme, sage and marjoram can also be sown early.

A further sowing of many vegetables sown in February is a good idea to maintain continuity of supply. It is also possible to make sowings this month in a cool greenhouse – with a little bottom heat – whereas sowings made earlier in the year required a heated greenhouse. Sow into deep seedtrays for planting out when the weather conditions allow.

Summer cabbage and cauliflowers can be sown this month. Cauliflowers, in particular, are prone to fail if given a check in growth during the early stages. Therefore, sow direct into modular seedtrays to reduce root disturbance when they are planted out into the vegetable plot. There are many varieties to choose from, but some of the most reliable include cabbages such as 'Greyhound', 'Hispi', 'Golden Acre' and 'Derby Day' and cauliflowers such as 'All the Year Round', 'Snowball', and 'Snow Crown'.

To get a winter supply of celery you'll need to sow this month. A little bottom heat is needed, but this can be provided quite adequately in a cool greenhouse. Sow in seedtrays in the usual manner providing a temperature of around 16°C. When the seedlings are large enough, prick them out carefully in rows into deep seedtrays at least 2in (5cm) apart with 2in (5cm) between rows. In May harden them off ready for planting out when the soil conditions are suitable. Self-blanching varieties are not frost hardy and must be cropped during the autumn. Old stalwart varieties such as 'Hopkins Fenlander' or 'Giant White' are best if you want a winter harvest.

If you would like a supply of juicy cucumbers to fill your salad bowl all summer long choose all-female varieties like 'Femspot' 'Pepita', 'Monique' and 'Sigmadew'. Sow two seeds about ½in (1.25cm) deep into a 3½in (9cm) pot, placing the flat seeds on their edge to prevent rotting. Pots can then be placed in a tray for ease of handling and covered by a sheet of glass to protect them from foraging mice. Keep the temperature around 18°C and seedlings will appear within a week, so the pots need to be checked every day for the first signs of life. Once germinated, take off the glass and remove the weakest seedlings from each pot. Then place the remaining seedlings in good light out of direct sun. As plants fill the pot, pot them on into 5in (12.5cm) containers before being planted out.

Sow sweet peppers in a seedtray. Aim to maintain a temperature of around 18°C. They quickly germinate and as soon as the first true leaves appear they can be potted on singly into 3½in (9cm) containers filled with potting compost. Harden off in May for planting out in June.

Aubergines (egg plants) sown in February can be potted on by the end of the month before they, too, are hardened off and planted out. It is still not too late to make a sowing if the February batch failed or was forgotten.

During the first couple of weeks of this month sow tomatoes for growing in an unheated greenhouse. Use a propagator to maintain a germination temperature of 18°C. Later in March further sowings of tomatoes can be made, but this time for cropping outside. The seed is large enough to sow singly and should be spaced 2in (5cm) apart in a seedtray filled with compost. As soon as the first true leaves on each seedling start to cross over or touch their neighbours in the seedtray, prick them out individually into 3½in (9cm) pots containing a potting compost. Water and feed the plants regularly and space the pots to allow free air circulation as the plants grow. By the end of April or early May the plants will need hardening off to be planted out in early June as the first truss of flowers starts to show colour.

Tomatoes sown in January for early cropping will require potting on into 5in (12.5cm) pots this month. Again, space the plants to let air circulate.

Planting

Cucumbers sown in February will now be large enough to plant out. The simplest method is to grow two or three plants in a growing bag. However, cucumbers can also be grown in the border soil. Prepare a bed in the greenhouse border early in the month by digging in plenty of well-rotted manure. Then build up a ridge of compost made from quality garden loam (sterilized) and well-rotted compost in a half-and-half mix. The ridge will need to be at least 18in (45cm) high and 2ft (60cm) long for every plant grown. Four or five plants will keep an average family self-sufficient in cucumbers throughout the summer.

Raise the temperature to at least 18°C before planting. When the young cucumbers are 6in (15cm) tall place them 2ft (60cm) apart along the ridge, providing each with a cane for initial support. Lightly firm and water well.

Cauliflowers sown in the autumn need to be hardened off ready for planting out as soon as conditions allow. It is most important not to check the growth of these plants because this can cause them to 'button' later on. That is, the curd will not develop beyond a button sized inflorescence. Therefore, lift plants with the utmost care with all roots intact. If you sow in modular seedtrays or peat pots this problem is largely avoided.

Fruit

Pollination

Those peaches and nectarines being grown in a cool greenhouse will be blossoming this month and so will again need hand pollinating and disbudding like those grown in heated greenhouses last month (see also February, page 50).

Grape vines started into growth in February will be blossoming this month and will also need hand pollinating using a soft paintbrush (see also page 69).

Late March sees the first strawberry flowers open in the heated greenhouse. Temperatures should be raised to 15°C. Hand pollination will again be necessary, using a soft brush; or dab them with cotton wool, otherwise subsequent fruit can be misshapen through poor setting. Water as necessary from now on as fruits begin to swell, but take care not to wet the crown of developing fruits.

Damping Down

Peaches and nectarines in a heated greenhouse will need watering and damping down daily after the fruits have set. Fruit thinning may well be necessary, but don't get carried away just yet since there is often a natural fruit thinning during April when many set fruit wither and drop off in a late cold snap.

APRIL

April is full of surprises as far as the weather is concerned. This month often brings hail, snow, sunshine and showers all in one month. Warm days and freezing nights make greenhouse gardening difficult. The middle of the month usually brings the characteristic sunshine and showers, but thunderstorms, too, can prevail so cautious ventilation is essential.

Greenhouse Briefing

Check heaters and ventilators.
Apply shading where necessary.
Check for pests and diseases.

Flowers

Sow annuals, biennials and perennials.
Sow primroses, polyanthus and pot-grown primulas.
Divide border dahlias.
Plant achimenes and amaryllis.
Stop chrysanthemums.
Repot house and greenhouse plants.

Vegetables

Sow melons, cucumbers and tomatoes for outdoor cultivation.
Sow sweetcorn, marrows, courgettes, runnerbeans and French beans.
Space early tomatoes.
Plant cucumbers and melons in an unheated greenhouse.

Fruit

Start vines in an unheated greenhouse.
Pollinate early starters.
Thin peaches and nectarines.
Pollinate strawberries.

General Management

April is often a month of conflicting interests with some plants requiring constant heat and others needing to be hardened off. In a large greenhouse this can be achieved by sectioning off areas with insulative bubble plastic, but in smaller ones it's much more difficult. A simple answer is to invest in a frame that can be given bottom heat in the form of soil-warming cables. Use this to harden off plants destined for the garden by gradually reducing the growing temperature and increasing ventilation. This will leave the greenhouse free for heat-demanding crops.

Alternatively you can take advantage of the temperature variations that occur within even a small greenhouse. For instance, those plants that need hardening off can be left under the influence of the cool air spilling through the ridge vent, saving the warmer greenhouse staging for seedlings and other tender subjects. This system, though, takes a lot more looking after and checking – requiring several maximum/minimum thermometers to help with this.

Heating is becoming less critical at night as the frequency of freezing temperatures lessens. However, it's easy to become complacent. Whatever the weatherman says, check the greenhouse every day to make sure all is well.

Ventilation becomes easier to sustain and, in fact, is essential to keep temperatures down during mild, sunny spells this month. Just keep using the ridge vents, though, and don't be tempted to open anything lower down since it could spell disaster. Aim for a maximum daytime temperature of about 21°C.

Shading is sometimes necessary in April, but only the temporary kind. Bubble matting is particularly useful at this time of year because it gives partial shading during the day and prevents cooling at night. Just pin it up on the south-facing side to keep out the strongest rays.

Watering will be more critical as many plants get into top gear as far as growing is concerned. Those still in small pots or yet to be pricked out of seedtrays are particularly vulnerable, so they must be checked each day.

With the new growth on many plants comes the threat of pest and disease attack. Check all crops as they are being watered for signs of damage or indications of other problems. Pests like aphids and red spider mite can build up in numbers very quickly if left unchecked.

Hanging Baskets

A wide range of hanging baskets is available these days. Which you choose will largely be a matter of personal preference. However, do check to make sure the supporting chains and ring (as well as bracket) are strong enough to cope with the considerable weight of a full, watered basket. Small baskets and wall mangers never do very well because the tiny amount of rooting medium dries out too quickly and is difficult to water satisfactorily.

Watering can be made easier by buying a basket that incorporates a drip tray or saucer. Better still, buy one of the plastic versions with solid walls, although they can look a bit out of place in a cottage style garden. The more traditional wire hanging baskets do dry out quickly but this can be offset, to some extent, by placing an old saucer in the base or lining the basket with polythene.

PLANTS FOR HANGING BASKETS

Name	Comments
Ageratum	Neat plants with powder-blue flowers all summer.
Alyssum	Flowers profusely from June to September.
Begonia	'Pink Avalanche', 'Pendula Chanson Mixed' and 'Basket Mixed'.
Campanula isophylla	Vigorous trailing plant producing star-shaped blooms.
*Chlorophytum	Plantlets weigh down elegantly arching flower stems.
Coleus	Fascinating mixture of leaf colours.
Fuchsia	Elegant bell-shaped flowers set against dark-green foliage.
*Hedera (ivy)	Evergreen trailer which provides year-round pleasure.
Helichrysum petiolatum	Arching stem of hairy grey foliage.
Impatiens	Spectacular variety of colours throughout the summer.
Lobelia	Trailing varieties like 'Blue Cascade' and 'Cascade Mixed' are best.
Nemisia	Many flowers in bright and showy colours.
Petunia	Compact plants that flower freely all summer.
*Pelargonium	Zonal varieties add height and ivy-leaved trail.
Tagetes	Extremely free-flowering in shades of orange.
*Tradescantia	House plant that provides interest to a summer basket.
Verbena	Flowering from June to October in a range of colours.

* Plants that will tolerate drought periods between waterings.

Planting

Stand the basket in an empty pot to stabilize it. Before planting up a wire-mesh hanging basket it must first be lined with a 1in (2.5cm) layer of sphagnum moss or a man-made liner. Sphagnum moss looks best, especially early in the season when the pendulous plants haven't had time to cascade over the sides. Then put in the polythene lining or saucer to help with moisture retention. Cover the base with potting compost, firming lightly to exclude air pockets.

If plants are to be grown from the sides as well as the top of the basket then they must be planted as the basket is being filled with compost. Tease a hole in the sphagnum moss lining about 3in (7.5cm) from the basket rim, then manoeuvre the plant through the mesh from the inside and set the rootball into the potting compost. Cover with compost and firm. Repeat this process until the basket sides are planted up.

Then fill the basket with potting compost to within 2in (5cm) of the rim. Starting at the centre, plant up the basket. Top up with compost so there is a 1in (2.5cm) watering gap below the rim, then mould the compost surface into a concave shape for easy watering. Alternatively, sink one or two holed yoghurt cartons into the compost. Either method allows water the time to be absorbed by the compost every time it is applied.

Flowers

Propagation

Early in this month there is still bound to be a great demand for space with many savings still to be made and earlier sowings waiting to be hardened off. Furthermore, many other greenhouse subjects will now be demanding more and more space, particularly where early tomatoes and cucumbers are being grown.

It's still not too late to sow most of the annuals, biennials and perennials recommended for March. It's a good idea, therefore, to check through those early sowings for failures. Damping off fungi can be a problem, wiping out whole seedtrays of seedlings. There is still time to make amends if a second batch is sown now. Of course, any seed being sown in succession will already be covering batch failures. Check the planned sowing programme with the seedlings now growing apace in the greenhouse. It is easy to forget to sow whole batches or mislay seed packets between house and greenhouse.

Where damping off has become a problem give each seedtray a drenching with 'Cheshunt Compound' fungicide. Also make sure all seedtrays and pots are thoroughly cleaned before re-use. Don't neglect plant hygiene with seedlings.

A second sowing of many annuals can be made later this month for use in the greenhouse and to supplement the display outside as the early sowings start to fade.

Primroses and polyanthus, that are most welcome during the dreary weeks in early spring, need to be sown now, since better germination is obtained when the seed is just ripe. Prepare a seedtray or pan of sieved peat-based seed compost and press the surface quite flat, leaving no holes or bumps. Water compost by standing container in water, then allow it to drain thoroughly. Add dry silver sand to the seed packet and mix well. This will act as a spreading agent when the dust-fine seed is sown. Scatter the sand/seed mix thinly over the surface of the compost, then lightly dust them with more silver sand. Place a sheet of glass and a newspaper over the seedtray to keep the seed moist. Maintain a temperature of 16°C in a shaded position until the first seeds have germinated. Sowings of several greenhouse primulas to be grown as pot plants can be mae this month. *Primula kewensis* ('Yellow Perfection'), *P. obconica* ('Gigantea Mixed', 'Blue Agate'), *P. sinensis* ('Revue') and *P. malacoides* ('Bright Eyes') are all worth trying. Sow in the same manner as primroses and polyanthus for a colourful display in the winter.

Zinnias need to be sown now in a temperature of at least 16°C, but preferably a temperature around 18–21°C. They greatly resent root disturbance so they will require to be pricked out with great care into modular seedtrays. Plants can later be potted on into 3½in (9cm) pots without upsetting their sensitive root system. Harden young plants off in May for planting out later that month – peat pot and all.

Cuttings

If earlier cuttings have failed or if there is a need for something to fill a colour gap in mid to late summer then it is still possible to take cuttings of plants like salvias, geraniums and fuchsias. Where the failure has been caused by a disease then this must be cleared up before new cuttings are taken.

Division

There is still time to propagate border dahlias by division to increase the stunning summer display (*see also* March, pages 52–53).

Planting

Achimenes can still be started into growth at a temperature of about 16°C. Fill a 5in (12.5cm) pot with a peat-based potting compost and space six to eight grub-like tubers over the surface. For a really stunning display try planting achimenes in a hanging basket to produce a cascade of pure white, red or pink all summer long.

To maintain a succession of eye-catching blooms, a batch of hippeastrum bulbs can be delayed by not planting them until the middle of April. Pot a single bulb into a 5in (12.5cm) container filled with potting compost. Water sparingly until signs of growth appear, then water

Fig 55 Aphelandra.

Fig 56 Crossandra.

more freely as the flowerbud pushes upwards. Feeding is important from this point on and must be continued after the flower has faded until the leaves start to turn yellow. Then stop feeding and reduce watering slowly to nothing to allow the plant to go into its dormancy period.

Resting

Cyclamen plants that are coming to the end of their flowering cycle will need feeding until the leaves start to yellow, then stop feeding and reduce watering slowly to nothing. The dry corms are then ready for storage until the autumn.

Repotting

Many house and greenhouse pot plants will require repotting this month. The repotting process is straightforward enough, but deciding whether a particular plant needs moving into a larger pot is not so easy. If an actively growing, healthy plant is potted on too early it can do more damage than if left to get a little pot bound. The answer is to err on the side of caution.

Once a plant appears to have filled its pot, knock it out and check the root system. If the roots have not completely filled the compost then leave, but where roots have started curling around the bottom it's time to repot.

HOW TO REPOT

1.   Water plants thoroughly, then leave for an hour or two before re-potting.
2.   Select a pot slightly larger than the first.
3.   Cover the base with a layer of peat-based potting compost and place the plant in the centre to check the planting level.
4.   Tip new compost around the rootball, firming as you go to remove air pockets.
5.   Top up with compost so there is a fine covering of the rootball. Firm lightly and water.

67

Fig 57 Schefflera, 'Umbrella Tree'.

Vegetables

Propagation

Melons, cucumbers and tomatoes for an unheated greenhouse or for planting outside can still be sown this month. The large-seeded melons and cucumbers can be sown two per pot (the weaker seedling later removed) on edge in 3½in (9cm) pots. The tomatoes should be sown at 2in (5cm) intervals along rows 2in (5cm) apart in a seedtray filled with seed compost.

Sweetcorn, marrows, courgettes, runner beans and French beans should also be sown now for planting outside later next month. Sow seeds singly in 3½in (9cm) pots filled with sowing compost. Cover with ½in (1.25cm) of compost and water well. Place a sheet of glass over the pots to prevent attention from mice and maintain a temperature of about 16°C. Harden off next month and plant out after the threat of late frosts has gone.

Fig 58 Sow large melon seeds on edge to prevent rotting.

Spacing

Tomatoes sown in January and February will now be growing rapidly and will need spacing out on the staging to prevent a check in growth or drawn plants. Plant out into border or growing bag when colour can be seen on the first truss of each plant.

Plants to be grown out of doors will need hardening off towards the end of the month ready for a good spell of weather in May.

Regularly remove any sideshoots that appear during this period by pinching the soft growth between forefinger and thumb. Bush varieties should be left to their own devices.

Tomatoes sown earlier this month will need potting on by the end into 3½in (9cm) pots filled with potting compost.

All tomatoes will be growing rapidly, so special attention should be paid to their water requirements. Don't let the temperature get too high either, since lanky growth is of little use.

Planting

With luck, young cucumber plants sown early in March will now be at the four-leaf stage and be ready for planting into cool or unheated greenhouses by the end of this month or the beginning of May. Prepare the bed in the same manner as described for early cucumbers, (see also March, page 63).

When healthy melons have developed their fifth leaf they are ready to be planted either into a prepared bed or a growing bag. Bring the growing bag into the greenhouse a few days before planting up so it can warm in the spring sunshine. Securely fasten several wires about 12in (30cm) apart to the greenhouse frame to provide support. Plant up the melons and stick a sturdy cane by each, tying the tops of the canes to the first wire.

Once settled, the melons grow away quickly and will probably need training before the end of the month. Tie the main leader to the cane guiding it to the first wire. Pinch out the leading shoot just above the last wire and tie in lateral shoots to the horizontal wires. These should then be pinched out when they've developed their fifth leaf. Throughout this period of rapid growth the plant will benefit from a humid atmosphere, so regular damping down of leaves and floor are worthwhile. Provide a little shading on very warm, sunny days, but give as much light at other times – temporary shading is necessary. Water and feed regularly.

Fruit

For grape vines being grown in an unheated house it is now time to start them into growth. Do this by closing down the vents and increasing day and night temperature. Dormant buds will then begin to swell and break by the end of the month. Untie the vine's stems (rods) from their supporting wires and bend them over so that the tips are just off the ground. The rising sap will then not rush straight to the terminal bud – encouraging even shoot development down the stem rather than leading shoots breaking away vigorously. Water thoroughly and damp down each day.

Those vines in heated greenhouses will have already been started (see also January, page 43) and the stage they have reached will depend on when the greenhouse was closed down as well as the subsequent temperatures and humidity.

Pollination

Vines started in March will now be in flower and so will need pollinating. Ventilate the greenhouse more freely as blooms begin to develop, to reduce the humidity. Do not spray overhead and try to keep air circulating.

The method of pollination will depend on the variety of vine being cultivated. Some, such as 'Black Hamburg' and 'Foster's Seedling', need only a generous tap or good shake just before midday to get sufficient pollen distribution. Others need a good deal more time with a rather tedious process of visiting flowers

69

individually with a soft paintbrush. This transfers the pollen in much the same way as insects do outside.

Thinning

January and February starters will have passed this stage earlier in the spring and, with luck, be showing fruits of previous labours. These fruits will need thinning so that they have a chance of developing into something usable (*see also* May, page 77). Water and feed as required.

Many early peaches will have rapidly swelling fruits. If good-sized fruits are required then some judicious thinning will probably be necessary. Pick off misshapen or stunted fruitlets. Then remove awkwardly growing fruits – those pressed against stems, wires or the greenhouse structure. Thin slowly over a period of weeks to get best results. Stop when there are about two fruits per square foot (metre) of vertical area covered by the tree.

Fig 59 Thin peaches by removing the smallest fruit.

Strawberries

Strawberries will also be in need of hand pollination this month (*see also* March, page 63) and any fruits not developing evenly should be removed early on to channel all the plant's energy into the good fruit. Thinning may be necessary.

MAY

The risk of late frosts still persists right through this month, so cautious hardening off and planting out are essential. The weather is generally less predictable, so keep an eye on forecasts since a late cold snap can ruin all your efforts in the garden.

Greenhouse Briefing

Prepare beds for hardened-off bedding.
Check for pests and disease.
Water and shade where necessary.

Flowers

Harden off bedding and other plants destined for the garden.
Plant out bedding.
Sow cinerarias.
Prick out seedlings as they become large enough.
Pot on rooted cuttings.
Plant out chrysanthemums.
Put freesias, nerines, lachenalias and arum lilies to rest for the summer.
Train fuchsias.

Vegetables

Harden off sweet peppers and aubergines.
Plant tomatoes in unheated greenhouses.
Train early cucumbers.

Fruit

Train and pollinate vines and thin early starters.

General Management

Much of the work associated with the greenhouse this month is outside in the garden – preparing areas for hardened-off, greenhouse-raised plants; clearing beds, borders and the vegetable plot as well as refurbishing tubs, troughs, hanging baskets and windowboxes.

It is also worth keeping a check on pests and diseases that will threaten to get a grip on various crops this month. If you keep problems down in the garden there is less likelihood of them spreading to the softer, more susceptible crops under glass.

Slugs can be a real problem about this time with young, soft plants being exposed to the big wide world. Before trying to combat them, however, scan the garden to see if there are any piles of rotting debris lying around. These moist, cool hideaways are ideal for slugs, so any dead or dying organic matter should be dispatched to the compost heap with haste.

May often sees the first really hot days of the year and so precautions must be taken to protect susceptible plants. This is complicated somewhat since the first couple of weeks can also see frosty nights that catch out the unwary gardener. Protect plants on sunny days with temporary shading material. It is still too early to erect any permanent cover since overcast days can be dreary indeed. Netting materials on the outside of the greenhouse, or adjustable blinds on the inside, are ideal and can be used on cold nights to insulate the greenhouse.

Heating is needed less now, but on the nights it is required it is critical. It is important, therefore, to check the heater regularly through this month. Gardeners who rely on paraffin will be having sleepless nights on those occasions that the heater is considered unnecessary. Paraffin heaters will also be wasteful on nights when a couple of hours heat is needed because they will be burning all night long.

Ventilation will not be so much of a problem this month. It will be possible to ventilate most days and even a little at night. Use the roof vents only at night – not utilizing side vents except on very warm, relatively calm days. Cold draughts can still cause problems.

Watering will remain vitally important throughout May with the increased periods of sunshine and high temperatures coupled with vigorous growth. Many plants will need watering every day but by no means all. Therefore, a check on each plant will be necessary each day – a rota will soon surface. Vigorous plants like tomatoes, melons and cucumbers will need a lot of water as will early vines, peaches and nectarines, to swell their developing fruit. Also check pot plants and seedtrays, since their limited volume of growing medium will dry out very quickly. Here watering several times a day will be needed.

There are a number of automatic or semi-automatic watering systems on the market that are worth considering if you do not have the time available to concentrate on the demanding spring and summer greenhouse (see also August, page 91).

Constantly scan all crops for outbreaks of pests and diseases. In particular, check the undersides of tomato and cucumber leaves for whitefly and red spider mite (see also Pests and Diseases, pages 121 and 123).

Clear debris from the greenhouse after the frantic sowing and potting season. Collect together used labels, pots and seedtrays ready for cleaning and storing.

Most plants in the greenhouse, indeed throughout the garden, will be in rapid growth and so require regular feeding.

Flowers

The clearing of beds and borders for bedding should be carried out at the beginning of May to take pressure off greenhouse and frame space as quickly as possible. Many bedding plants will already be hardening off in the upper reaches of the greenhouse or in the cold frame. Before the month is out nearly all will be planted out in the garden and growing away.

Fig 60 Campanula.

With bedding being moved out early in the month, areas of greenhouse staging will start to be clear ready for the potted seedlings and rooted cuttings from last month. Where temporary staging becomes redundant later in May, take it down to make way for the dominant summer crops of tomatoes, cucumbers and melons.

Propagation

Sow cinerarias now for a kaleidoscope of winter colour. These pot plants are covered in tight clusters of flowers held clear of a compact backdrop of foliage. Sow seed thinly on seedtrays filled with sowing compost and cover lightly with compost. Maintain a temperature of around 13°C – not usually a problem at this time of year. Check seedtrays daily for the first signs of germination, then move to a well lit position out of direct sunlight. To get continuity of colour from December to April, several sowings must be made until July.

Pricking Out

Primulas, calceolarias and cinerarias sown last month will be ready for pricking out in May. Wait

72

until the seedlings can be handled safely before placing them individually into 3½in (9cm) pots filled with a peat-based potting compost. Water well and place in a light, but shaded, position.

Potting On

Rooted cuttings of perpetual-flowering carnations, pelargoniums, fuchsias, coleus and the like, will need to be potted on when they have outgrown their 3½in (9cm) pots. Move them on into 5in (12.5cm) pots using potting compost. Water in well and return them to their shaded position on the greenhouse staging. Ventilate freely and maintain a temperature of about 15°C. Once the plants are established, pinch out growing tips to encourage bushiness. Then harden off any plants destined for the great outdoors. Any plant material removed when stopping can be trimmed up just below a node, lower leaves removed and inserted into a gritty compost as cuttings. Rooting is quick at this time of year so that these cuttings may well require potting up individually in 3½in (9cm) pots next month.

Planting

Earlier chrysanthemum cuttings – those taken during January, February and March – and potted

Fig 61 Aechmea.

Fig 62   Regal pelargonium.

on for planting out of doors will be ready for hardening off in a cold frame. If there is no space available, then by the end of the month it will be safe to place them in the shelter of a south-west facing wall protected on cold nights with hessian sacking.

Once hardened off they are ready to be planted out in their flowering position. Select a sheltered site and prepare it by digging in well-rotted farmyard manure to a well-dug plot. Where quite a number are to be grown mark out a bed 4ft (1.2m) wide and put a stout post in each corner. Then lay a sheet of 5in (12.5cm) mesh pea and bean netting over the bed, attaching it to a wooden crossbar at each end with a length of strong wire woven through each side of the netting and running from one crossbar to the other. Fix the wire securely to the crossbars so the netting is held out flat. Place one crossbar over the posts at one end and then using the other crossbar roll the wire and netting up until, when pulled really taut it can be slipped tightly onto the two posts at the other end of the bed. Push both crossbars down to ground level.

Plant shallowly in three staggered rows. Then, as the plants grow and develop, slip the crossbars up the posts to support them. Water after planting and water and feed regularly from next month onwards. If, however, only a few chrysanthemums are to be grown then they can be placed in the borders or as a single row and supported individually with a stout bamboo cane.

Hardy perennials raised from seed or cuttings will now be ready for planting out into the garden once hardened off. Alpines, too, can be set out.

Potting

Chrysanthemums to be grown in the greenhouse in late summer will need to be potted on into 5in (12.5cm) pots as they fill their 3½in (9cm) containers. During the summer they will need potting on again into 8in (20cm) pots and placed in a sheltered spot in the garden to enjoy the warmest weather. For each repotting it is best to use a loam-based compost such as J.I.P. No. 3 which will provide a stable base.

Chrysanthemums that were stopped last month will have, by now, produced a lush crop of sideshoots (breaks). Where more than three or four breaks have shot up, then the weakest should be pinched out as soon as possible. However, where prizes at the local horticultural show are the aim then restrict these breaks to two per plant.

Fig 63   Regal pelargonium.

Resting

Several precious winter and early spring-flowering greenhouse plants will now be coming to the end of their season. Freesias, for instance, will need to be rested during the early summer months for them to perform the following winter. Water well while the plants remain in flower, but reduce this slowly to nothing as they begin to die down. Prevent compost from becoming dust dry.

Many bulbous plants like nerines, lachenalias, arum lilies and cyclamen also need a restful summer. Again, reduce watering after the last flowers fade, allowing the leaves to yellow and die back naturally. The bulbs should be left in the dry compost and pot until they are started off into growth again during August. Store arum lilies on their sides under staging away from drips, but leave nerines and lachenalias in a sunny spot where they can ripen.

Training

Fuchsias being trained as standards will have reached the tops of their canes and will need pinching out if not already done. Subsequent breaks from buds lower down the stem should be pinched out at the fifth pair of leaves to produce a well-balanced head. Fuchsias grown in pots and baskets will need pinching out to encourage a bushy well-structured plant.

Hanging baskets will need watering more frequently now that plants have become established and are beginning to grow away.

Vegetables

Harden off sweet peppers and aubergines that have established themselves in 3½in (9cm) pots. Plant out later in the month in milder areas and you will need to support each plant with a bamboo cane. Plants being grown under glass should be potted on or planted into a growing bag — two or three plants per bag is usual depending on volume.

Fig 64 Remove the growing tip of the fuchsia to encourage the head to develop.

Planting

It is time to plant tomatoes when the majority of the plants are showing colour in the first truss of flowers. Tomatoes should be set out 18in (45cm) apart in the border and spaced equally in a growing bag — the number per bag will depend on the volume of compost it contains. Aim for a temperature around 10°C at night, rising to between 16°C and 18°C during the day.

Ventilation should be given when necessary to keep the temperature down on warm, still spring days. At night, leave a top vent open when the weather is particularly mild.

Tomatoes set out in an unheated greenhouse at the end of last month could well be looking a bit blue after a few cold nights. Protect plants with sacking or newspaper at night until chilly spells end.

Plant cucumbers in unheated greenhouse, if not already done (*see also* April, page 69).

Training

Plants develop quickly in the long, warm days of spring and soon some form of training will need to be adopted if they are not to get out of hand. A couple of weeks after planting they will need extra support. This can be given in two ways; either tie them up to individual canes using raffia; or attach them to an overhead wire with a length of string.

Raffia ties should be every 6in (15cm) or so up the stem and must be secure without being constricting – remember the tomato stem will swell at the base as the plant grows. Tie the top of the cane to an overhead wire for stability. Where growing bags are being used, then it might be necessary to invest in one of the specially designed support systems that uses the weight of the bag to give the crop a steady support.

String training can be used for tomatoes grown in border soil or growing bags. It is simply a matter of having one end looped securely around the base of the plant – again with plenty of room in the loop – while the other end is tied to an overhead wire using a secure slip knot.

As the tomato plant grows the string is carefully wound around the stem in a spiral. One complete revolution every 6in (15cm) or so, is enough to give overall support. This training can usually be done without untying the slip knot on the overhead wire – simply manoeuvring the growth around the string. However, where

Fig 65 Flowers on a tomato plant.

growth has exceeded expectations then the slip knot can be carefully slackened, the plant trained and the knot retightened again.

For long season (early) tomatoes this system could not take account of the height of the tomato plant after several months of growth – perhaps as much as 12ft (4m). In these circumstances another string training system is required. This involves having a piece of string long enough to take account of so much growth (12ft (4m) long), then attaching one end to the tomato plant as before and the other to a special S-hook (available from specialist suppliers). The excess string at the beginning of the season is wound around this S-hook until all the slack is taken up. The S-hook is then hung over the overhead wire. The training of the tomato plant early in the season is exactly the same as before, but when the plant reaches the overhead wire a little string (about 1ft (30cm)) is unwound from the S-hook and the hook returned to the overhead wire about 6in (15cm) to one side. This causes the

Fig 66   Support tomato plants by tying to bamboo canes.

tomato plant to lean to one side. Repeat this several times and the plant stem is slowly layered. Keep the stem off the ground by tying it to a low-level wire.

After the plant has been trained it is time to remove all sideshoots. Don't do this before training just in case there is an accident and the growing point is broken out – if this happens before sideshooting, then the most vigorous sideshoot can be trained up instead of the broken growing point.

Train early cucumbers throughout the month (*see also* June, page 81). Keep the temperature high – at least 21°C at night. Ventilators should be shut down most of the time to maintain this temperature, only being opened on very warm days. Always shut vents before nightfall to capture the warm solar-heated air inside the greenhouse.

Since cucumbers require such warm and humid conditions they don't fit in with the growing of tomatoes that like it drier and more airy. However, it is quite possible to grow them side by side if you are prepared to compromise your growing technique.

Pollination

Hand pollination isn't always necessary but for a good set on the first truss it's worth visiting each flower systematically with a soft paintbrush. This should be done on warm days before midday.

Shading

By the end of the month shade the greenhouse with either a proprietary shading whitewash that needs to be applied to the glass, or hang up a shading fabric or blind.

Watering

Melons need to be watered with care since these plants suffer from rotting around the base of the stem. For this reason many gardeners sink an empty plant pot into the border compost about 6in (15cm) away from the melon plant and fill this several times each watering. This system also ensures that water gets deep into the border compost.

Melons still require a warm humid atmosphere and so damping down must be done with great care. They also require shading from the sunniest weather.

Fruit

With the increased power of the sun, new vine growth can suffer from scorch, so light shading should be provided. Small greenhouses are most vulnerable because they warm up most quickly.

Pollination

When the new shoots on grape vines reach 18in (45cm) long many will have produced flower trusses. Let the shoot develop until two leaves have unfolded beyond the truss and then pinch it out. Those without flower trusses will also need pinching out.

Vines that were started last month will now need hand pollinating, so go around each flower with a soft paintbrush and transfer pollen (see also page 69).

Thinning

Early starters in heated greenhouses will soon be in need of thinning. Aim to leave at least one good-sized bunch of fruit per foot (30cm) run of wire. The first step is to remove weaker trusses in close proximity to other better developed bunches. Also discard those trusses in a poor position; those next to the glass, as well as those that are too high, too low or just awkward to get at.

Once this is done turn to the bunches remaining to shape and thin them (see also page 82). To thin grapes with ease it is necessary to have the right tools. A specialist pair of grape-thinning scissors are best, but any sharp, pointed, small yet sturdy snips or scissors will do. A short prop (stick with a forked tip) is also required to support and separate the bunches that are being thinned. It is important to avoid touching the grapes at all costs because handling destroys the fruits' bloom – the dusty white covering to each grape – and will thus weaken their natural defences.

Peaches and nectarines will be rapidly swelling this month. They should be watered thoroughly and damped down daily once the fruits have set. Take care when cultivating soil under peaches and nectarines because their surface roots resent disturbance of any kind. Thin fruit if this has not already been done (see also April, page 70). The earliest started trees will have ripening fruit this month when damping down must be stopped.

Raise the temperature for strawberries when fruit have set to around 20°C during the day and 15°C at night. Continue to water and feed plants as necessary.

JUNE

The threat of night frosts is over in many areas by the beginning of June. In exceptional years, though, they can catch out the unwary gardener by appearing as late as the second week. In the north, of course, freezing night temperatures can be a reality until the middle of the month every year.

Greenhouse Briefing

Keep a check on temperatures by regulating the ventilation.
Put up shading where necessary.
Check watering requirements daily.

Flowers

Sow Primula malacoides, P. sinensis and P. kewensis.
Sow cinerarias and alpine calceolarias.
Take softwood cuttings.
Pot on rooted cuttings as necessary.

Vegetables

Train tomatoes and cucumbers.
Sideshoot tomatoes.
Water and feed carefully.
Harden off aubergines, sweet peppers, marrows and ridge cucumbers.

Fruit

Thin grapes.
Water and feed peaches, nectarines and strawberries.

General Management

The long sunny days will cause the temperature in the greenhouse to rise rapidly in the mornings and stay hot all day. Rapid rises in temperature, and falls for that matter, should be avoided by careful ventilation early in the morning as well as later afternoon. Where an automatic vent opener is on the shopping list, it would be worthwhile buying it this month so that it can be fitted before the ventilator has become less accessible.

There will, of course, be the added benefit of having an automatic vent throughout the summer. Furthermore, if July is hot then the stock of automatic vents on sale will be in short supply as demand rises.

Hot days will require free ventilation both top and bottom. Extra ventilation can be gained by opening the door or, in extreme cases, removing one or two panes of glass.

Vents should also be protected from birds – the last visitors a gardener wants to see in the greenhouse. Netting is a cheap and reliable solution, but make certain it doesn't foul the workings of the vent.

Shading will be necessary this month for many greenhouse plants. Either apply a proprietary shading whitewash designed to be painted directly onto the outside of the glass or put up a shading fabric if not already done. This can be anything from a cheap plastic mesh to the more expensive blinds. Blinds, of course, are preferable because they can be rolled up or down as the need arises.

Watering is by now the most time-consuming job in the greenhouse. Hours can be spent each day checking and watering each plant. Where large quantities of water are required on a regular basis, as for tomatoes, cucumbers, melons and fruit trees under glass, then watering will be a tiring and often despised task. In addition, some crops such as tomatoes suffer when they become water stressed – encouraging problems like blossom end rot that render whole trusses of fruit useless.

Feeding once a fortnight will be required by most plants in the active growth phase. Select a high-potash fertilizer for fruiting and flowering crops – a tomato fertilizer is ideal. For leafy plants choose something with a balance of the nutrients nitrogen, phosphorus and potassium (NPK).

Flowers

Propagation

There is still time to sow *Primula malacoides* for a colourful display this winter – try varieties such as 'Bright Eyes' in lovely combinations of carmine, rose, white, pink and purple or 'Unwins Formula Mixed' that embrace shades of pink, lilac, red and white. Further sowings of *P. kewensis* and *P. sinensis* can also be made. Scatter the seed thinly in a shallow seedtray filled with compost. Cover them very lightly and place the seedtray in a temperature of about 16°C to achieve germination. Since the seed is so near the surface it is important to cover the seedtray with a sheet of glass or place it inside a polythene bag to prevent it from drying out. Lay a sheet of newspaper over the seedtray and keep it away from direct sunlight. Remove this paper as soon as the seed starts to germinate and place the seedtray in a lightly shaded position.

When the seedlings are large enough to be handled they need to be pricked out singly into 3½in (9cm) pots filled with potting compost. Move them out to the cold frame to harden off.

Sow another batch of colourful cinerarias for autumn flowering. Sow thinly into a seedtray filled with seed compost and maintain a temperature of around 13°C. Prick out cinerarias sown last month when they are big enough to handle safely. Don't prick out too many though – it is easy to get carried away!

Alpine species of calceolarias need to be sown this month as soon as the seeds are ripe. Prepare a seedtray of sowing compost and sow thinly by adding dry silver sand to the seed packet to act as a thinning agent. Place the seedtray in a greenhouse or cold frame where the seed will germinate. Pot-grown calceolarias for greenhouse display during the winter can still be sown this month if not already done.

Clearing out of the greenhouse of all potted up young plants destined for the garden can be completed this month. Stack empty pots and seedtrays ready for a cleaning binge later in the year. Remove the last of the temporary staging and give the rapidly growing greenhouse border plants, like tomatoes and cucumbers, all the space you can.

Cuttings

Many garden plants can be propagated by summer-struck cuttings. The warm long days means they can root quickly ready for potting up in a matter of weeks. Much of the growth available, however, is soft and fleshy so it needs to be protected from the ravages of the sun and dry atmosphere.

The simple solution is to stick cuttings directly into a closed atmosphere away from direct sunlight. The high humidity will prevent the cuttings wilting, so giving them time to root.

Many herbaceous perennials like chrysanthemums, dahlias, lupins and delphiniums can be propagated this month while the young shoots are soft. Select a healthy non-flowering shoot and cut it cleanly from the parent just above a leaf joint. Remove the lower leaves and trim to just below a leaf joint so that the cutting is about 4in (10cm) long. Stick the cutting in a gritty compost where it should root.

Where a garden frame is not available then a simple alternative can easily be made. A wooden box with a sheet of glass on top will do, or even a pot with a cheap clear plastic top can be effective where only a few cuttings are planned. Once filled with cuttings, the box frame should be watered well, then closed and shaded. Keep an eye open for outbreaks of fungal diseases, spraying where necessary with a systemic fungicide containing benomyl.

Many rock plants can be propagated from cuttings taken this month.

If you want a lavender hedge take cuttings now. Select 3–4in (7.5–10cm) sideshoots during this month or next and remove the lower leaves and soft growing tips. Fill a 5½in (14cm) pot with a gritty cutting compost and insert them in an inch (2.5cm) or so apart around the edge of the pot. Put a couple of short split canes in the pot,

then place it in a clear plastic bag. Keep in the greenhouse out of direct sunlight and the cuttings will root within four or five weeks.

Leaf cuttings of streptocarpus and saintpaulias can be taken this month (see also Propagation, pages 33 and 34).

Potting On

Rooted cuttings of pelargoniums and fuchsias that have now outgrown their 3½in (9cm) pots should be potted on into 5in (12.5cm) containers using a potting compost.

Similarly, pot on any perpetual-flowering carnations if you have not already done so. As soon as they have produced about eight pairs of leaves, pinch them back to five. When sideshoots are produced from the leaf joints, they too will need to be stopped so that the plants will break again.

If you leave some sideshoots to flower they will bloom earlier than those left alone. Using this method you can achieve an almost continous show of blooms throughout the winter months. Give plants adequate shading during the hottest weather and place a stake in each pot to provide support. Do not feed perpetual flowering carnations until the flowerbuds show, but keep well watered and damp down the greenhouse floor on scorching days.

Hardening Off

The last of the chrysanthemum cuttings taken in March will now be ready to harden off before being planted out into the garden.

Greenhouse azaleas can be placed in a shady sheltered spot outside later this month for their summer holiday. This helps ripen the shoots to promote flowering next year. Plunge the pots into soil so they don't dry out too quickly and water as necessary.

Where chrysanthemums are being grown for their large blooms they will need careful watering and feeding this month. Those for a garden display of flowers should have their growing tip

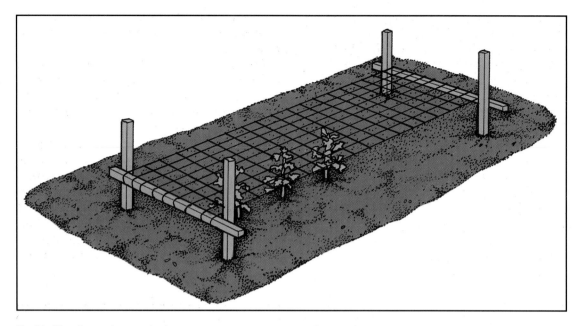

Fig 67   The chrysanthemum bed.

pinched out, when shoots from the first stopping are at least 12in (30cm) long. This will encourage many flowering stems, producing a multitude of smaller blooms.

Spray varieties will need pinching out again before the end of the month. Greenhouse chrysanthemums should be stopped for the first time at the end of the month, with spray varieties second pinching carried out in the middle of July.

Vegetables

Continue to train the early sowings of tomato plants by either adding new ties where raffia ties are being used or winding the string around new growth where the string method is being employed.

Removing sideshoots from tomatoes must be carried out as a matter of routine – at least once and preferably twice a week this month. Remove small sideshoots by holding the plant beneath a leaf joint with one hand and bending the sideshoot over at 90 degrees, first one way and

Fig 68   Remove tomato sideshoots after the plants have been trained.

Fig 69 Flowers on a cucumber plant.

then the other. The sideshoot will snap out cleanly.

Larger shoots missed on previous occasions should be cut out using a sharp pruning knife. If there is any disease in the house then dip your knife in a fungicidal solution like 'Bordeaux Mixture' between cuts.

The most important shoots to remove are those directly below a flower truss since they are often the most vigorous and if left to grow will take sap flow away from the truss, reducing its yield. Check for pests and diseases while removing sideshoots.

Training cucumber plants up secure wires must continue through this month. Tie the stem loosely, but securely, to the wire using loops of string. Stop the cucumber plants by pinching out the growing tip when they reach the roof.

Systematically stop all lateral shoots back to the second leaf joint and pinch out all male flowers (those without the swelling behind the flower). Of course, this will be much less of a problem on the so-called all-female varieties. Remove female flowers from the main stem on all varieties.

The laterals of melons planted in frames will need to be stopped as they reach the corners of the frame. Subsequent sub-laterals will produce male and female flowers that will need pollinating (see also April, page 69).

Aubergines and sweet peppers under glass need staking this month, if not already done. Place a cane about an inch (2.5cm) from the main stem. Spray the flowers with water when they open to help fruit set. Water as necessary and feed every fortnight with a liquid fertilizer. Both these crops are compatible with cucumbers so they can all be grown together at one end of the greenhouse.

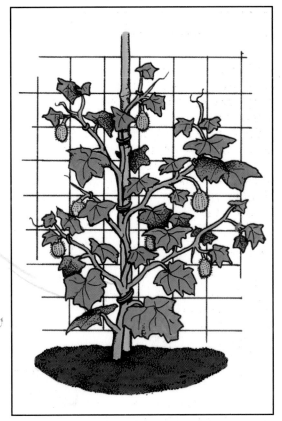

Fig 70 Tie melons securely to support.

Pollination

As new trusses develop on tomato plants, you can systematically go round the greenhouse and lightly tap each truss to distribute pollen, although this isn't always necessary. Some growers like to damp down the crop in order to help pollination. Whatever the method, it is best done just before the warmest part of the day.

Feeding

Continue to feed all tomato plants using a high potash tomato fertilizer. Sowings made at the beginning of the year will now be carrying rapidly swelling and ripening fruit. Watering is of critical importance now – applications every day may be necessary if the weather is warm. Ventilation is important, too, so open vents and even the door on hot sunny days, and top vents on still, mild evenings.

Growing bags containing greedy crops like tomatoes, cucumbers and melons will need regular feeding at least once a week all month. Liquid feeds are far better than powder because they are instantly available to the plants. With such large amounts of feed being applied to so little compost there is going to be a risk of salt building up and damaging roots. To avoid this ensure that the bag is watered heavily with pure water to wash the excess salts away.

Cucumbers will need shading if not already provided, so apply a proprietary whitewash or hang one of the various netting materials available. Damp down the greenhouse and plants each day to keep up the humidity but restrict watering to just a couple of times a week. Those grown in mounds on border soil will require top dressing with compost when roots start to show through the surface.

Reduce the humidity for the melons as the early fruits start to swell. Don't let the daytime temperature fall too low, though. Remember to water and feed with care as necessary and keep an eye open for pests and diseases.

Harvesting

Harvest as soon as cucumbers have reached a suitable size. Never leave fruit on a plant to get old since this stops younger ones from developing.

Hardening Off

Move out vegetables such as aubergines, capsicums, marrows and ridge cucumbers sown in April to be hardened off, if not already done. These can then be planted out as soon as space becomes available.

Fruit

Thinning

Grape bunches will need to be thinned out in two stages. First make sure you have a suitable pair of scissors and a supporting stick with a forked tip to hold bunches apart while they are thinned (see also May, page 77) – do not touch the fruit with your hands because if the bloom is spoilt it reduces the fruit's natural defences.

Check the centre of the bunch and remove most of the grapes. This allows air circulation through the bunch. Then remove small and imperfect berries. Finally, the bunch should be thinned to give each berry remaining enough room to swell to full size.

The top or shoulder of the bunch will need less thinning than the centre if you are to preserve the classical shape of a bunch of grapes. Tie the shoulder of the bunch to a supporting wire using several loops of string.

Feeding

Check peaches and nectarines regularly to make sure they have enough water while the fruits are swelling. Start feeding this month and carry it right through until the end of August.

Those with ripening fruit should not be sprayed, but ventilate both top and bottom,

Fig 71 Thin developing bunches of grapes so that they can swell properly.

JULY

The greenhouse in July is a hot and humid place with a mixture of flowers and vegetables coming into their main season. Greenhouse climbers such as bougainvilleas, *Plumbago capensis*, lapagerias and the ever popular passion flower are all blooming profusely this month.

Greenhouse Briefing

Careful ventilation is essential to control greenhouse temperatures.
Put up permanent shading.
Water as and when necessary.
Check for pests and diseases.
Send heaters off to be serviced.

Flowers

Sow cinerarias and alpine calceolarias.
Sow stocks and mignonette (*Resada odorata*).
Prick out primulas and other seedlings.
Taking cuttings of *Hydrangea petiolaris*, abelia, forsythia and many other garden shrubs.

Vegetables

Water and feed plants as necessary.
Train tomatoes, cucumbers and melons.
Check for pests and diseases.

Fruit

Thin grapes.
Feed and water all fruit.
Harvest ripe fruit.
Check strawberry plants for greenfly.
Select strawberry runners for forcing next year.

General Management

Keeping the greenhouse cool enough is the main problem in July. Opening vents both top and bottom as well as leaving the door open is often not enough on those hot, still, balmy days. Removing

providing the temperatures don't fall too low. Keep a special look out for red spider mite while damping down has been abandoned since this pest thrives in a drier atmosphere.

Water and feed strawberries as the fruits swell. If there has been a very good set it might well be worth thinning them to improve their size. All misshapen, badly set fruit should be removed and discarded. Keep the greenhouse well ventilated on warm sunny days, but don't let the temperature drop too low. Keep an eye open for pests and diseases.

As the first fruits start to colour up it is important to keep the atmosphere dry so ventilate freely. Stop feeding at this point.

Fig 72   Gloxinia.

glass panes, as described in June, is a laborious job that nobody wants to do and on still days this has very little beneficial effect.

Forced ventilation is the only real answer – some form of extractor fan built into the end wall of the greenhouse to push hot air out and draw cool air in. Air movement is important because it will reduce the incidence of disease.

Keep a close check on the temperature in your greenhouse, particularly if it is small and heats up quickly. Here a maximum/minimum thermometer is a good investment and will indicate when the greenhouse precautions against the sun are working. More shading is often required this month even with sun-lovers like tomatoes needing protection against those unrelenting sun rays. Check the shading material you have

already erected to see that it is intact or; if you have used the whitewash type, not wearing thin or flaking off.

Outside shading is really needed this month because this type keeps the greenhouse cooler than the internally erected types. Roller blinds, sheets of netting or whitewash are all suitable.

A watering routine will now be well under way, so little extra has to be added to the remarks for last month. But don't become complacent because plants will soon suffer if they run short of water – reducing yield and developing other associated problems. Check each plant at least once a day, but on hot days two or even three waterings will be necessary for those plants with limited root run. Feeding at fortnightly intervals should also be continued to keep actively growing plants happy. Hungry plants such as tomatoes require feeding every week. Pests and diseases will be eager to take over the greenhouse and its bounty of crops if you are not careful. So check all the plants thoroughly as often as possible for any signs of damage or pest and disease presence. Red spider mite, thrips, whitefly and greenfly continue to be a nuisance and caterpillars may well put in an appearance. Placing a net over ventilators to keep out butterflies will eliminate the caterpillar problem, but make certain the net doesn't foul the workings of the vent.

Heaters will become completely redundant this month and can be removed from the greenhouse. Don't just throw them in a corner of the potting shed for the summer but give them a thorough overhaul. Check for faults, sending machines away for any repairs so that they are ready for use in the greenhouse by the end of September.

Flowers

Propagation

Try some winter-flowering pansies to brighten up the greenhouse display by sowing now outside in a prepared seedbed or in a coldframe. Germination will take only a couple of weeks and young seedlings will soon be ready to be pricked out. The variety 'Floral Dance Mixed', will, given reasonable weather, flower right through until the following spring. It is free-flowering with ruby, violet, white and yellow forms all available.

Cinerarias can be sown to continue the succession this month (see also June, page 78) and those sown last month will be ready for pricking out into 3½in (9cm) pots using a potting compost. Even established seedlings will need plenty of shade now.

Alpine calceolarias will be producing ripe seed this month, so they need to be sown as soon as possible for best germination. Place the seedtray in a cool greenhouse or frame where the seeds will germinate. Seeds sown in June will need

pricking out as soon as the seedlings are large enough to handle safely. Put them singly into 3½in (9cm) pots filled with potting compost and return them to the cold frame.

If you want a glorious show of heavily scented blooms in the greenhouse during the winter then make a sowing of stocks outside in a prepared seedbed this month. Choose a sheltered spot and keep well watered.

A winter display of mignonette. *Resada odorata*, can be sown this month onwards. This valuable pot plant produces long, slender spikes densely packed with flowers that have a delicious morning and evening fragrance. Varieties like 'Fragrant Beauty' and 'Crimson Fragrance' tell their own story. Sow half a dozen seeds in a 5½in (14cm) pot, thinning them to leave the strongest three or four.

Cuttings

Many flowering garden shrubs can be propagated, by cuttings taken this month. Choose healthy semi-ripe shoots. That is, a shoot of current year's growth, soft at the tip but starting to ripen – producing a woody outer layer – at its base. Select non-flowering shoots about 4in (10cm) long where possible and remove them from the parent plant with a heel of woody stem.

Trim the heel with a sharp knife so that there are no snags and remove lower leaves from the cutting. Dip the cut tip of each cutting in hormone rooting powder. Next fill a 5½in (14cm) pot with a cuttings' compost or make a well-drained rooting medium from peat and perlite, in a half-and-half mix. Water well. Stick the cuttings around the edge of the pot using a narrow dibber or pencil to make the holes. Keep cuttings from wilting by placing in a mist unit or putting each pot into a clear plastic bag. Some cuttings are more difficult than others to root and so some form of bottom heat may be needed. Soil-warming cables in a frame or propagator on the greenhouse staging is the obvious remedy. Suitable subjects include abelia, forsythia, iberis,

Fig 73 Mini-Rose 'Sunblaze'.

lithospermum, solanum, pittosporum, potentilla, pyracantha, philadelphus, escalonia, kolkwitzia, lonicera, cotoneaster, caryopteris and weigela.

Hydrangea petiolaris can also be increased by selecting healthy new growth and taking 3in (7.5cm) cuttings. Take off the lowest pair of leaves and trim the cutting to just below the leaf joint. Remove the softest growing point to prevent wilting and stick in a well-drained gritty compost in a cold frame. When the cuttings are rooted pot them up.

Pricking Out

Prick out sowings of pot-grown primulas and calceolarias for winter flowering. Place them individually into 3½in (9cm) pots filled with potting compost.

86

Disbudding

Disbud early chrysanthemums this month, i.e. remove all the buds and sideshoots that develop from leaf joints down the stem, so that only the terminal bud remains. Spray varieties are not disbudded.

Planting

Check resting cyclamen tubers because they'll soon be shooting away. Where tubers are getting too big for the pot they can either be potted on into a larger container using a fresh compost or divided.

As soon as the buds start to show cut the tubers into two or three pieces, using a sharp knife. Make sure each section of the tuber has a healthy, plump bud. To protect against fungal infections it's a good idea to dip the cut surfaces in a fungicidal powder such as 'flowers of sulphur'. Pot up the tuber sections in a potting compost so that the crown is standing proud of the surface. Water well and place in a cool, shaded position.

Vegetables

Continue to water and feed all tomato plants regularly – watering every day if required. Hand pollination by tapping the trusses lightly will also

Fig 74   Feed and water tomatoes regularly.

Fig 75 *Fruit forming on a tomato plant.*

reach full size. Once laterals have finished fruiting they should be removed and a new one trained in its place to extend the cropping season.

Ventilate on hot days, not letting the temperature rise above 32°C and aiming for about 25°C. Don't lose all the humidity otherwise there will be outbreaks of damaging red spider mite.

Melons will need supporting with a net as they swell. This should be dangled securely from an overhead supporting wire. Melons are ripe when the surface around the stem begins to crack.

Whitefly

Whitefly can be a real problem in the greenhouse because they are difficult to control at egg and larval stages. To overcome their resistance to chemical control it is necessary to make repeat treatments every four to seven days for about three weeks. In this way all the whitefly in the greenhouse will have been treated at adult stage at least once.

Fruit

Propagation

Strawberry plants for next year should be selected from runners now being produced on garden plants. Several varieties are suitable for forcing including 'Gorella', 'Pantagruella', 'Red Gauntlet', 'Cambridge Vigour' and 'Rival'. Choose strong, healthy runners and peg them down into 3½in (9cm) pots, buried nearly up to their rim in the soil and filled with compost.

Thinning

Late-started vines will need their first thinning this month if it hasn't already been carried out (*see also* June, page 82).

Grape vines often need a second thinning about a month after the first. This involves checking the bunch over and removing any small or malformed berries. Then check through the

be of benefit throughout the month as new flowers open up. Also, keep sideshoots under control; they don't need a second invitation to fill the greenhouse with foliage. Train plants as necessary.

Training

Stop tomatoes as they reach 6in (15cm) above the top supporting wire to encourage the quick development of fruit so they have all ripened by the autumn — it takes about eight weeks for tomatoes to develop and ripen at this time of year. However, if you want tomatoes after this period then let the plants grow up to the eaves.

Lower leaves will start to yellow and should be removed. In fact, at this stage it's worth removing leaves up to the first truss to let air circulate around the fruit. Some people also thin leaves — that is, remove one of the three leaves that develop between trusses.

Damping Down

Maintain a humid atmosphere for cucumbers by damping down the greenhouse and plants each day. Continue to harvest cucumbers as they

Fig 76   Peg out strawberry runners into 3½in (9cm) pots filled with compost.

bunch to ensure that there is enough room for their final weeks of development and growth. Check that the string tying the bunches to supporting wires isn't constricting and add any extra ties where necessary.

Feeding and Watering

Careful watering and feeding is necessary while the vine is in active growth. Give large amounts of water at well-spaced intervals, giving gallons of water each time to get moisture deep into the soil. Don't water little and often.

Continue to feed and water peaches and nectarines as necessary, but leave off damping down and ventilate using both top and bottom vents. Ripening will be more rapid on warm sunny days. Check regularly for red spider mite – particularly on the underside of leaves where they are just visible as tiny red-brown or buff specks.

Harvesting

Harvest peaches and nectarines as soon as they are ripe – they turn a yellowish hue and give slightly when pressed lightly in the palm. Strawberries need to be well ventilated as they colour up. Don't feed, but continue to water as necessary, taking great care not to splash the berries since this encourages botrytis or grey mould. Harvest as soon as they are ripe.

Keep an eye open for greenfly that will plague strawberry plants given half the chance. If an outbreak of botrytis does occur, then remove the affected fruit and spray the rest with a fungicide containing benomyl.

89

AUGUST

In good years or bad years, depending on your point of view, August can often bring many of our hottest days. When the weather doesn't break, close, hot days will persist, and this makes effective ventilation in the greenhouse difficult to achieve.

We are now well into the main growing season and the greenhouse is chock-a-block with plants threatening to get out of control. Colourful greenhouse climbers that are still giving their best include bougainvilleas, Plumbago, capensis, lapagerias, passion flowers and *Cobaea scandens* (cathedral bell). Again the annual climbers like *Thunbergia alata* (Black-eyed Susan), which has orange plate-like flowers with purple eyes, and *Ipomoea* (morning glory) with its shining sky-blue trumpet blooms, are performing well and not showing any signs of slowing down.

Greenhouse Briefing

Keep the greenhouse cool by careful shading and ventilation.
Careful watering throughout the month.

Flowers

Prick out sowings made last month.
Sow schizanthus, *Primula malacoides* and stocks.
Sow cyclamen.
Take softwood cuttings of pelargoniums, fuchsias, verbenas and penstemons.
Start off freesias, lachenalias, arum lilies and nerines.
Rest gloxinias.

Vegetables

Sow lettuce for winter cropping.
Harvest tomatoes, cucumbers, sweet peppers and aubergines.
Train, feed and sideshoot tomatoes.
Train and feed cucumbers.

Fruit

Water and feed vines carefully.
Harvest peaches and nectarines.
Harvest strawberries.
Pot up newly rooted strawberry runners.

General Management

Keeping the greenhouse cool enough is again the main problem during August. Use ventilation and shading to best effect as described in July to keep those desiccating sun rays at bay. Ventilate using both roof and side vents during the day, but still needing only roof vents at night. Watering must be given as often as required. This can mean two or three times a day for plants in small containers. Plants in growing bags, like tomatoes and cucumbers, will be producing fruit all month and will require large amounts of water.

Holidays are another problem that face all but the most dedicated greenhouse gardeners during the summer months — who will only take them when the greenhouse is dormant. August is the most popular time for taking holidays and yet there is a lot of work to be carried out in and around the greenhouse. What can be done?

Well, sympathetic neighbours are the obvious answer — greenhouse sitters who are willing and capable of holding the fort while you are away. But it's a lot to ask and how many of us have neighbours that are interested in gardening?

The only answer is to simplify matters. Reduce the management to checking a thermometer, switching on a button and turning on a tap. That's certainly straightforward enough, but how can we get all that needs to be done in the greenhouse down to just a few simple operations?

Automatic vents will be of great advantage and shading can already be in place, so that leaves watering. You can water automatically, but constant checks must be made to ensure the system is working well — critical for those plants in pots with a limited root run.

Many plants can be removed from the scorching

black polythene

capillary matting

polythene

Fig 77 Fully automatic watering system.

greenhouse and into a sheltered spot in the garden. Make a plunge bed in a shady area. Water thoroughly before you leave and all will be well when you return. Plants that will not adjust to the climatic change must be kept in the greenhouse. Make a cheap, yet reliable, semi-automatic watering system using capillary matting. First, get a sheet of poythene and lay it on level staging; then cover it with a layer of capillary matting material long enough to dangle over one end. Fix some form of reservoir at the end of the staging; it must be wide and shallow and not below the staging's surface because the capillary action can only lift water a couple of inches, or so. Therefore, water more than 2in (5cm) below the level of the staging will remain in the reservoir.

The dangling end of the matting should then be placed in the reservoir. Wet the matting all over and fill the reservoir with water. Place another sheet of polythene – black this time – on top of the matting to prevent the growth of algae. Then space the pot plants on top of this.

Once this is completed, take each plant off in turn and cut a hole slightly larger than the bottom of the pot in the polythene. Return each pot plant to the staging and water from above to start the capillary action. Where a mains supply of water is available and the reservoir large enough to take a ballcock then this system can be made completely automatic.

Set the system up at least a week before the holiday to iron out last minute problems so that it's working like clockwork before you go. Do remember, though, that pots must not have crocks for drainage, nor rims on their bases because the capillary action cannot bridge these gaps and the pots will not receive any water.

Flowers

Propagation

Many spring-flowering greenhouse pot plants can be sown this month. Sow thinly into a seedtray filled with sowing compost and keep at around

91

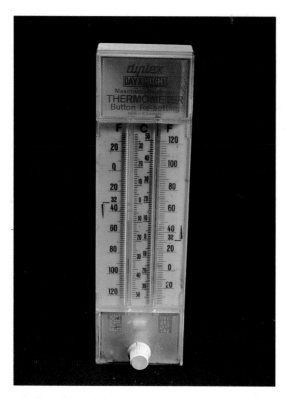

Fig 78 Check greenhouse maximum/minimum thermometers regularly.

The winter-flowering pansies can be sown now in seedtrays or seedbeds outdoors or in a cold frame. The wide range of colours and delicate scent last well into spring. Sowings made last month should be pricked out as soon as they are large enough to handle safely.

If you want early spring-flowering clarkia in the greenhouse you'll need to sow the seed in a well-prepared seedbed this month or next. Pot up seedlings into 3½in (9cm) containers to grow on for a few weeks before moving them into their final 5½in (14cm) pots. Place in a cool greenhouse over winter so that they are ready for flowering in February or March.

May-flowering nemesia can also be produced if seed is sown now. Aim to get three seedlings in a 6in (15cm) pot of potting compost by sowing five seeds and thinning out the weakest. Pinch out the remaining plants when they are well established to encourage bushy growth.

Schizanthus 'Star Parade' is another flowering pot plant recommended for small greenhouses. The compact orchid-like blooms produce outstanding displays for early summer. Sow thinly in a seedtray and cover lightly with compost this month. Kept at a temperature of around 10°C, they soon germinate. They can be potted up into 3½in (9cm) pots filled with potting compost as soon as they can be handled. Again, these benefit from being pinched out when they are well established to obtain thick bushy growth that support the weighty blooms in the spring.

Cyclamen in shades from deep and rich purple to white flushed with pink bring warmth to the coldest rooms during the winter months. Mid-August is the best time to sow cyclamen for flowering at Christmas the following year. Space seed about 1in (2.5cm) apart in a seedtray filled with sowing compost. Cover the seed and place in a greenhouse or cold frame. Prick out seedlings when they fill the tray – second leaf stage – into 3½in (9cm) pots of compost. Start last year's corms by cleaning off remaining debris and repot using fresh compost. Water sparingly until new growth is apparent.

Stocks are one of the most popular flowers

13°C until germination has taken place. Cover with a sheet of glass and newspaper and place in a warm position. When the germinated seedlings are large enough to handle they should be pricked out into 3½in (9cm) pots filled with a potting compost. Place in a cold frame out of direct sunlight. A final sowing of cinerarias can be made now. For small greenhouses try the compact variety 'Gay Time Mixture' that produces an abundance of colourful blooms on a 10in (25cm) high plant. Also worth trying is 'Amigo Mixed'.

Sow *Primula malacoides* if you want to produce whorls of stunning blooms on slender stems during the early spring. The variety 'Pastel and Stripes' will also provide a delightful fragrance. Other good varieties include 'Bright Eyes' and 'Marie'.

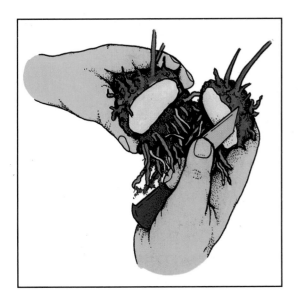

Fig 79 Use a sharp knife to divide cyclamen tubers so that each piece has at least one plump bud.

Fig 80 Select a strong, healthy non-flowering Pelargonium shoot and cut it cleanly from the parent plant.

sold for cultivation in the garden and they can also be grown as a pot plant in a heated greenhouse. They are available in several forms, in a range of colours from pink to red to purple as well as yellow and white.

'Beauty of Nice' stocks and 'Brompton' stocks both grow to about 18in (45cm) high, 'East Lothian' stocks make about 12in (30cm) pot plants, whereas the rather more vigorous 'Giant Excelsior Column' stocks attain a height of 24in (60cm).

Sow 'Beauty of Nice' stocks now for winter colour and the others for flowering in spring. Scatter the seeds thinly in a seedtray filled with a sowing compost. It is worth watering with 'Cheshunt Compound' to prevent damping off disease. Place prepared containers in a cool greenhouse or cold frame to germinate.

'Brompton' stocks are selectable and this means that it is possible to eliminate nearly all single-flowered plants at seedling stage. This is achieved by removing the seedlings with dark green leaves and potting up only those with light green leaves.

Cuttings

Pelargoniums can also be propagated this month by taking softwood cuttings. Both the zonal and ivy-leaf bedding types are easy to increase in number by selecting healthy non-flowering shoots about 5in (12.5cm) long. Using a sharp knife, cut them cleanly from the parent plant without leaving a snag. Trim each shoot to just below a leaf joint to produce a 3in (7.5cm) cutting, then remove the lower leaves. Dipping in hormone powder is not normally necessary. Insert prepared cuttings either around the edge of a 6in (15cm) pot or individually into 2½in (6cm) pots containing a sandy compost. Do not let the cuttings wilt before putting them in the pot and keep out of direct sunlight afterwards. Water well and place in a sheltered spot.

Other tender plants such as fuchsias, verbenas and penstemons can also be propagated from healthy non-flowering shoots. Take a 3–4in (7.5–10cm) cutting and trim just below a leaf joint, remove lower leaves and dip base in a hormone rooting powder. Insert around the edge of a 3½in (9cm) pot filled with a gritty compost, then water and place in a closed frame or seal in a plastic bag. For best results maintain a temperature around 18°C. By the end of September the cuttings will have rooted and can be potted on individually into 3½in (9cm) pots.

August is an ideal month for taking cuttings from many showy greenhouse plants including abutilon, *Cissis antartica* (kangaroo vine), citrus, croton, datura, drasinia, hibiscus, *Passiflora* (passion flower), philodendron and verbena.

Select young, firm, healthy shoots about 4in (10cm) long and trim below a leaf joint, using a sharp knife. Trim off lower leaves and dip cut end in hormone rooting powder. Insert around the edge of a 3½in (9cm) pot filled with gritty compost and place in a closed frame.

Cuttings taken last month will soon be showing signs of rooting by becoming fully turgid and even putting on fresh growth. They must now be removed from the plastic bag or propagator and hardened off to the less humid greenhouse atmosphere. After a week or so they'll need potting on individually into 3½in (9cm) pots using a

Fig 81   Gerbera.

Fig 82 Hibiscus.

potting compost. They are best kept in a cold frame over winter rather than being planted out in the garden borders.

Many more garden plants will be producing suitable material for semi-ripe cuttings this month including ceratostigma, escallonia, fatshedera, hebe, hypericum, jasmine, philadelphus, sambucus, viburnum and weigela (*see also* July, page 85).

Planting

Christmas-flowering freesias can be obtained if you start plump healthy corms now. Their delicately branching sprays make ideal cut flowers for the festive season and fill the house with a lovely scent. Place about six or eight in a 6in (15cm) pot of potting compost so that they are about 1in deep. Water and place in a cool greenhouse or frame or in a sheltered spot outside. Keep watering sparingly until the first growths are apparent. Those pots started outside must be brought indoors before the first cold snap of early autumn.

Elegant lachenalias, better known as the Cape cowslip should be potted up this month as well. In pots or hanging baskets their strikingly colourful

95

Fig 83 *A small greenhouse is an ideal growing area for the amateur gardener.*

bell-like blooms make a superb display. Again, place six bulbs in a 6in (15cm) pot filled with potting compost, then cover with a further inch or so. Water well. Don't water again until growth is visible. Keep in a cool ventilated greenhouse or frame. Alternatively make use of your spring hanging baskets by cleaning them out and filling them with lachenalias.

The much underrated nerine (the Guernsey lily) is another bulb ready to be started into growth after the summer's rest. *N. bowdeni* produces up to ten rich pink large florets that make excellent cut flowers. Pot up one, two or three bulbs into 3½, 4 or 6in (9, 10 or 15cm) pots respectively so that the neck of the bulb is visible. Place in a cold frame, water sparingly until the first foliage appears. Bring into the heated greenhouse or living room to flower. Take care not to overfeed, otherwise they'll produce a lot of leaves at the expense of blooms.

Resting

Early-starting gloxinias will be showing signs of yellowing. Reduce watering slowly to nothing, removing dead flowers and leaves regularly to prevert diseases getting a hold in the resting tuber. Store in a warm (12°C), dry place out of direct sunlight. Be decisive when throwing out tubers – only keep young healthy stock.

Vegetables

Propagation

Later this month sow a tray of the lettuce variety 'Kwiek' for planting out into the greenhouse border when it becomes vacant. Sow seed individually 2in (5cm) apart each way in a standard seedtray or in modular seedtrays filled with sowing compost. Plant out 8–10in (20–25cm) apart in early October as soon as the seedlings are large enough to handle. Where a minimum temperature of around 7°C can be maintained, varieties like 'Columbus', 'Marmer', 'Kellys', 'Pascal' and 'Ravel' can be sown to produce a succession of crisp heads all winter long. Sow 'Columbus' now to mature from the beginning of November onwards.

Harvesting

Harvest tomatoes all this month. Keep a careful eye on watering to ensure you don't get problems like fruit splitting and blossom end rot that are associated with erratic watering. Continue to feed, sideshoot and remove yellowing lower leaves as necessary. In very warm years actively growing tomatoes, cucumbers and melon plants in the greenhouse may well need watering more than once a day if you are to achieve the maximum yield possible. If this is not practical – if you are out at work, for instance – then it's worth investing in some form of continuous trickle irrigation. If you are growing in bags, then automatic irrigation is a great help in average summers, too.

It takes about eight weeks for fruit to develop, swell and ripen. So where tomatoes are being grown in an unheated greenhouse it would be a good idea to pinch out the growing tip to encourage those fruits already set to develop at full speed.

Fig 84   Remove male flowers from cucumber plants.

Continue harvesting cucumbers as they become available. Frame-grown cucumbers will now be available, so if you have a crop then remove the ageing plants from your greenhouse this month. If not, keep greenhouse cucumbers cropping by cutting out old laterals and training new ones. Remove plants that have finished cropping.

Feed and water through the month as necessary. Make sure the temperature doesn't get too high nor the humidity too low. Check whitewash shading to make sure it hasn't been washed off by summer rain.

Harvest melons. The skin around the stem on the melon starts to crack when they are ripe. You'll be in no doubt when melons are ripe because they fill the greenhouse with a sweet aroma. Place pieces of wood or tiles under rapidly swelling melons in garden frames to protect them from the soil.

Sweet peppers can be harvested when they start to sound hollow when tapped. If red fruits are wanted pick them when they are just starting to turn, then ripen them fully in the kitchen. You can, if you prefer, let them ripen to red on the plant but this will reduce subsequent fruit production considerably because the plant slows right down. Watch out for greenfly and whitefly, spraying where necessary.

Aubergines, too, will be ripening for harvest. Pick them as soon as they are ripe and don't be tempted to harvest more than eight fruits off one plant because size and time will be lost.

Fruit

Feeding and Watering

To get good quality fruit from your grape vines careful watering and feeding must be a priority throughout the growing and, in particular, the fruiting season. Water thoroughly once a week or so, increasing the amounts given in response to hot weather. Feed the vine thoroughly in the growing season with a fertilizer high in potash. Tomato fertilizer is ideal, given every other week while the vine is growing, starting just around flowering time.

Check shading, particularly if it's the whitewash type, in case its effect is waning.

Ties holding bunches of grapes should also be checked to ensure they are not constricting sap flow and are providing ample support.

Continue to feed and water peaches and nectarines as necessary. Those plants that have already been harvested can be sprayed daily again to increase humidity and to keep red spider mite and thrips at bay. Ventilate both top and bottom.

Harvesting

Harvest fruits as they become ripe. If you are lucky enough to have a glut of fruit, excess can be stored perfectly well in a cool place.

Harvest the last of the strawberries as they ripen and keep the atmosphere dry through good ventilation. Check fruit daily for outbreaks of grey mould, picking off any affected fruit. Water carefully as necessary.

Once plants have finished fruiting they are of

no further value, so should be consigned to the compost heap.

Potting On

New strawberry runners selected last month that were pinned down into 3in (7.5cm) pots filled with compost should now have rooted sufficiently to be liberated from their parent plants. Water and feed as necessary to produce strong healthy stock for next year. Later in the month they'll probably be ready for potting on into 6in (15cm) containers filled with a peat-based potting compost.

Place the plant to one side of the pot, with the growing point facing outwards. This will be helpful next year when the plants are fruiting since they will then dangle over the edge of the pot and not in the compost where they can become wet and rot.

SEPTEMBER

September sees shortening days, colder nights and the end of many summer-flowering greenhouse plants. Beautiful greenhouse climbers such as bougainvilleas, *Cobaea scandens*, passiflora, thunbergia and ipomoea all continue to bloom this month, but the display slowly tails off.

Pelargoniums and fuchsias are an inspiration to us all as they soldier on producing bloom after bloom. It's little wonder they are among Britain's favourites when they are such good value for money.

The petunias and streptocarpus are still blooming this month, but, again, their best days are now over.

Greenhouse Briefing

Overhaul heating equipment.
Careful ventilation and watering is becoming important.
Remove permanent shading.

Flowers

Sow hardy annuals.
Sow cyclamen.
Start cyclamen corms and arum lilies.
Start freesias and lilies in pots.
Pot up prepared bulbs for forcing.
Check cuttings.
Take cuttings of evergreens and bedding plants.

Vegetables

Water tomatoes and cucumbers carefully.
Harvest tomatoes, cucumbers, sweet peppers and aubergines.
Harvest melons when ripe.
Prick out lettuce.

Fruit

Check temperature changes in greenhouses containing ripening grapes.
Check for pests and disease.
Harvest peaches and nectarines.

General Management

As the summer nears its end the nights become distinctly colder and days shorten. Heating may be necessary during a cold snap and so all heating equipment must be overhauled at the beginning of the month. Check also that flues are clear and fuel supplies are readily available.

Ventilation will be used less frequently through the month depending on the weather conditions. In a warm spell both roof and side vents will be needed, but on cooler days ridge vents only will be necessary. Aim for day temperatures of about 15°C. At night the temperature will be dropping quite low so ventilate sparingly so that the greenhouse maintains a minimum of around 8°C. Damp down in the morning during warm spells and let the greenhouse slowly dry out towards the evening. Don't forget to close the vents a couple of hours before the sun goes down to capture the last of the day's heat.

Check the vents have not been distorted during the summer so that they sit snugly on their frame without gaping cracks. It is essential to seal leaky vents if you are to maintain a minimum night temperature without resorting to expensive heating.

Less and less shading will be required as the month progresses. Remove the permanent shading first so that the remaining temporary material can be removed and replaced according to the weather. Proprietary whitewash material can be removed with warm water and a scrubbing brush. It is important to remove all traces because light levels in the greenhouse during the winter can be critical. Only maintain a permanent shade over established shade lovers.

Reduce watering as temperatures drop and growth rates slow down. Take care not to overwater. Use an insecticide smoke to control late infestations of whitefly, red spider mite and aphids.

Plants which have stood outside during the summer will soon need to return to the greenhouse. Watch the weather forecast for cold snaps – particularly if it is windy – and move tender plants inside. Check them over carefully so that no pests or diseases are introduced unwittingly into the greenhouse.

Flowers

Propagation

Pots of heavily scented flowers in rich colours look stunning during dull winter days. Make sowings of half-hardy annuals such as 'East Lothian' stocks, 'Beauty of Nice' stocks, schizanthus, clarkia, godetia, calendula, larkspur, anchusa, nemophila and salpiglossis. Sow in a well-prepared seedbed now, if not already done. If sown last month, seedlings will soon be ready to be potted up into 3½in (9cm) containers and placed in a cool greenhouse to get established.

September is the last month for sowing the seed of large pot grown cyclamen. They will be ready to flower at Christmas the following year. The alternative is to sow in January or February

for small plants flowering at the end of the year. For best results soak for about twelve hours before sowing. Then space the plump seed about 1in (2.5cm) apart in a seedtray and cover lightly with peat. Place the seedtray in an airy, but warm and light, position out of direct sun. Wait until the seedlings are touching before pricking out individually into 3½in (9cm) pots. At this stage plant the tiny corms two-thirds proud of the compost surface and maintain a temperature of around 15°C.

Cuttings

Check cuttings to make sure they aren't wilting or succumbing to rot. Once rooted they should be potted up individually in 3½in (9cm) pots and placed in a cold frame or a cold greenhouse to overwinter.

Many evergreens can be propagated from semi-ripe cuttings this month. Select sideshoots of the current year's growth with firm bases showing slightly woody colouration. Sideshoots between 3–5in (7.5–12.5cm) long are best and should be pulled away from the parent plant with a heel (see also Propagation, page 33). Suitable subjects include Cupressocyparis leylandii, all types of chamaecyparis, thuja, taxus, picea, juniperus as well as Cryptomeria japonica.

It's worth noting that to maintain the prostrate habit of ground-hugging conifers it is necessary to select material from the sides and not sideshoots pointing skywards.

Cuttings can also be taken from many bedding plants and inserted directly into the prepared bed of well-drained compost – a half-and-half mix of peat and sharp sand – inside a cold frame with bottom heat.

Planting

Many greenhouse flowers that have enjoyed a summer's rest can be started into growth this month to fill the greenhouse with colour and fragrance, from Christmas onwards. Mature cyclamen, for instance, should be cleaned of any

Fig 85   Hydrangea.

dead, dry foliage. Repot into the old container using fresh compost. Water sparingly at first to encourage them to start into growth.

Arum lilies are ready for starting in September to produce those characteristic stately white blooms that surround a startling spiked yellow centre in early summer. Choose a pot to suit the number of rhizomes — between 6in (15cm) for a single swollen root and 10in (25cm) for up to five. Fill the base with drainage crocks before topping up with compost (J.I.P. No. 2). Set the rhizomes 2in (5cm) deep in the compost, firm and water. Stand pots outside in a sheltered spot until the middle of the month — later if the weather is mild. Move indoors before the first frost.

This is an ideal time to plant freesias for flowering around Christmas and into the New Year. Their branching sprays of sweetly scented blooms in a range of yellows, whites, pinks and purples are a real treat. Plant six corms about 2in (5cm) apart in a 6in (15cm) pot filled with potting compost. Cover with compost so that each corm is an inch or so deep. Water sparingly at first, increasing rations as growth develops. Freesias, too, can be left outside until frosts threaten.

There's still time to pot up your lachenalias (Cape cowslips) for their colourful bell-like blooms from December onwards. Space six bulbs in a 6in (15cm) pot equally and cover with 1in (2.5cm) of compost. Place in a cool and ventilated greenhouse or frame.

Lilies should be potted up singly in 6in (15cm) pots from now onwards. There are basically two methods. One way is to set stem rooting varieties deep into the pot, leaving plenty of space for top dressings of compost as the plant shoots and produces roots up its stem. Other lilies that do not produce roots from the stem should be potted up like other bulbs. Once potted, keep the pots in a cool place watering sparingly until growth shows.

Some lilies like *Lilium longiflorium* can be gently forced in a temperature of about 16°C when the established bulb will produce a flowerbud. Water and feed little and often until colour shows in the bud.

There is nothing better during a dull winter day

Fig 86   Begonia 'elatior'.

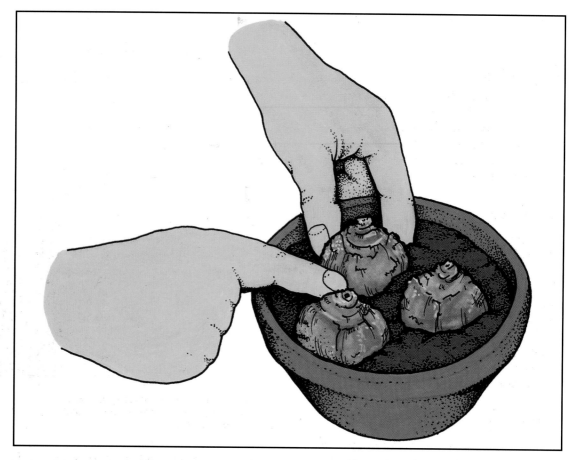

Fig 87   Don't force bulbs into the compost when planting.

than to grace the living room with a supply of beautiful daffodils. It is easy to achieve, but often forgotten.

Purchase bulbs that have been specially prepared for forcing. If you select containers without drainage holes then it is important to use proprietary bulb fibre if the compost is to remain sweet. Check that the compost is moist, but not too wet. Fill a container with compost to the level of the base of each bulb. Space bulbs around the container and then fill in gaps with more compost – don't fill the container with compost and then push the bulbs in.

Cover the bulbs so that their necks are just visible, then place them in a cool spot in the dark

to encourage root production and prevent the shoot breaking too early. The usual way of achieving this is to plunge the containers into a deep bed of peat or ashes outside. Cover in polythene to keep the worst of the weather off, but check that the pots don't get too dry.

Hippeastrums can be brought in now for Christmas flowering. The sizeable bulbs need a large pot, 6in (15cm) often being necessary. Fill pot with potting compost, then excavate a small depression to take the bulb so that it sits two-thirds into the compost. Water sparingly until growth becomes apparent, keeping it in a light, draughtproof spot. Maintain the temperature at around 15°C. Water well as the flowerbud emerges to be followed by dark green strap-shaped leaves.

Disbudding

It is important to disbud chrysanthemums if you require large single blooms. Remove all the lateral buds on the leaf axils leading to the terminal bud which is left to produce the bloom. Spray varieties need to have only the terminal bud removed.

Vegetables

Greenhouses heated to around 16°C through the winter can support a crop of tender French beans ready for Christmas dinner. Varieties like 'Limelight', 'Masterpiece' or 'The Prince' can be sown 2in (5cm) deep in a large pot – 10in (25cm) – filled with a peat-based potting compost.

The watering of tomatoes is still critical at the beginning of the month but shouldn't be quite as time consuming as it was last month. Remove the lower leaves to help ripen the remaining fruit.

Harvesting

Ripening and harvesting of tomatoes will continue throughout the month in the greenhouse. If night temperatures can be kept up then fruit can be harvested next month too. However, there will be a great demand for greenhouse space at and beyond the end of the month with all the tender containerized garden plants needing protection, so it is a good idea to take the last harvest of fruit at the end of this month.

All fruit that are starting to turn colour should be picked off and placed on a tray on the windowsill to ripen. Make a winter stock of green tomato chutney with the less advanced fruit.

Melons in frames will be ripening this month. Keep the atmosphere dry and reduce watering. Lift melons up to give them maximum light and protect them from cold snaps at night with sacking. Harvest when the skin of the fruit starts to crack around the stem.

Fig 88   Avoid cucumbers touching the soil or wet areas by placing a piece of wood or pad under the cucumber.

Sweet peppers and aubergines should be harvested throughout the month, although some aubergine plants will have been cropped bare and should be removed and discarded. Feed and water as necessary.

Pricking Out

Prick out lettuce seedlings when they are large enough to handle safely. Make further sowings for continuity of supply.

Fruit

Keep on top of your tipping back of new shoots arising from the grape vine. They must be cut back to the first leaf, otherwise they'll take over the greenhouse. Tendrils will also develop at an alarming rate and need removing as soon as you notice them.

Damping Down

As the first grapes start to ripen steps must be taken to reduce the risk of fruit splitting. Rapid changes in temperature and high humidity are thought to be the main culprits, provided adequate water has been given through the life of the crop.

Damping down should, therefore, be carried out in the morning and a roof vent should be left open an night to lower humidity and slow the early morning heating effects of the sun. Prevent uneven watering by giving the border a thick mulch.

Check the bunches for diseases and pests throughout the month, removing offenders as soon as they are noticed. Avoid touching the grapes.

Harvesting

Once bunches of grapes look ripe they will need to be left on the vine for anything from two weeks to a couple of months, depending on variety. This allows the sugars to form and therefore improves the taste.

Harvest any remaining peaches and nectarines as they ripen on the fruit trees started into growth late in the spring. Continue to ventilate the greenhouse so that the new wood produced this year becomes fully ripened. Try not to let temperatures fall too low, though.

Newly potted, rooted strawberry runners will be filling out their pots as they become established. Stand them in a sunny, sheltered spot. Spray the leaves each day and water as necessary.

OCTOBER

October is usually the wettest month of the year. It is a good time to start bringing in the remaining tender plants after their summer holiday in the garden since stormy and colder weather soon prevails.

Chrysanthemums in the greenhouse really come into their own this month. Decorative varieties with large, intricate blooms in a kaleidoscope of colours stand tall on 3ft (1m) stems. A fair amount of space is necessary, but the effect is quite spectacular when the crop is in full glory. Perpetual-flowering carnations complement the chrysanthemums; although not nearly so showy, their blooms have unmistakable appeal.

Greenhouse Briefing

Check heating equipment and thermostats.
Cut down on ventilation.
Water sparingly.
Close down part of the greenhouse if not fully utilised.

Flowers

Sow sweet peas for the show bench.
Prick out seedlings.
Rest tuberous begonias and gloxinias.
Last chance to start freesias.
Pot up spring-flowering bulbs.
Take conifer cuttings.
Label dahlias in the garden.

Vegetables

Harvest tomatoes and sweet peppers.
Sow lettuce in greenhouse for succession.

Fruit

Harvest grapes.
Ripen new wood on peaches and nectarines.
Water strawberries carefully.

General Management

Nights will be drawing in quickly and days shortening to provide precious little time for evening gardening. Temperatures will drop considerably this month with an increased threat of frosts at night. Aim to keep the greenhouse temperature above 7°C by the judicious use of heating and ventilation. Daytime temperatures around 12°C are easier to maintain, but some heat will inevitably be needed on cold damp days when the weather closes in. It's worth considering whether you close down part of your greenhouse for the colder winter months to save on heating bills. Partition off a section with a roof vent and a heat supply using polythene, or preferably bubble matting to give a good insulation layer.

Ventilation will be restricted to daytime only. On still, bright days open the vents a couple of hours after dawn and close them again a couple of hours before dusk. This will trap as much heat energy as possible from the sun and reduce potential heating bills. Ventilate more freely if the temperature rises above 20°C, but keep it to roof vents only – side vents will cause damaging draughts of cold air to sweep through the soft greenhouse plants. Greenhouses heated by non-flue gas or paraffin heaters will need to be ventilated to prevent the build-up of noxious fumes given off as a by-product of combustion. Water vapour, too, is produced and so this must be ventilated out to reduce the risk of diseases. Cold greenhouses containing hardy plants should be ventilated during the winter to lower the instance of moulds and mildews.

If you are intending to buy a greenhouse heater, buy this month before many tender favourites are lost to the winter weather. An electric heater such as a portable fan heater is useful to start with because it is simple to use, takes very little space and requires next to no maintenance. It also has the added advantage of being able to circulate the air which has a considerable depressing influence on outbreaks of fungal attacks. It also distributes heat in the greenhouse keeping all plants safe. Where only a few plants need to be kept from the icy clutches then it may well be more economical to invest in a heated propagating frame or propagator

rather than a heater. Water sparingly all this month, taking care not to splash sensitive plants like primulas and cyclamen.

Also check around the garden for any forgotten tender or half-hardy plants that need to be protected in the greenhouse to survive the winter. Check over the plants to remove yellowing leaves and catch outbreaks of diseases early. Control attacks by using a smoke cone containing either tecnazene or sulphur. Do not spray unless absolutely necessary.

Flowers

Delicate blooms in pastel hues on stiff, but slender, stems await anyone who sows sweet peas. If sown now, the plants will be well established early in the season allowing them to produce larger and longer displays than those sown in spring. This is the best time to sow if the blooms are destined for the show bench (see also January, page 38).

Fig 89 Mammillaria Solissi.

Fig 90 Sow sweet pea seeds singly in special tubes.

Cuttings

Continue taking cuttings of conifers until the end of the month and get well-rooted plants by late spring. This is not the quickest method of propagation, but it is simple and requires little after-case. Select sideshoots 3–5in (7.5–12.5cm) long – any longer and there is a tendency to dry out without rooting. The material should be of healthy growth and be free of all pests and diseases. Each sideshoot should be ripening well at the base where it joins the parent and when pulled off should come away with a short 'heel' of bark (see also Propagation, page 33).

Transfer pots of cuttings to a closed propagation case or cold frame where they will be able to root before drying out. Alternatively, place two short canes in the pot and place the whole thing in a polythene bag. The stakes will support the bag and prevent it touching the cuttings and rotting.

Water sparingly from now on and keep cuttings fairly dry during the winter months.

Try growing cuttings with a little bottom heat if you want them to root before winter. This can be achieved by soil-warming cables or a heated propagator. Remember, though, that although these cuttings are perfectly hardy, and indeed

Fig 91 Place pot into plastic bag to prevent cuttings from wilting.

need a winter rest period if they have been given bottom heat, they should be weaned off the heat slowly.

Pricking Out

Prick out sowings of half-hardy annuals made last month into 3½in (9cm) pots then place in a light, but cool, spot in a greenhouse or frame to get established. Water sparingly and open ventilators whenever weather permits. Earlier sowings which are now well established will need to be pinched out to produce sturdy potted specimens.

Rapidly developing cyclamen will also need pricking out individually into 3½in (9cm) pots as they become too big for the seedtray. Grow on at a temperature of around 15°C. Feed young growing plants of cyclamen, clarkia, schizanthus, cinerarias and primulas with a weak feed containing plenty of potash.

Resting

Tuberous begonias will now be starting to turn yellow to prepare for their winter rest. Reduce watering, allowing the compost to dry out. Place dry tubers in a cool, dry place until spring.

Gloxinias and hippeastrums can be treated in a similar fashion to begonias, except they prefer to be left in their pots during the resting stage.

Don't bother keeping gloxinia tubers once they've reached three years old.

Planting

October is just about the last chance to start freesias. Their superb branching, one-sided flower spikes are a refreshing addition to any greenhouse display. Plant six corms 2in (5cm) apart in a 6in (15cm) pot filled with potting compost. Cover with an inch more compost and firm lightly. Water sparingly until growth appears.

Fig 92   Kalanchoë.

Water and feed developing freesias, lachenalias, lilies and cyclamen. Autumn-flowering chrysanthemums in pots that were stood outside for the summer should be brought inside at the beginning of the month. Check over the plants for pests and diseases before bringing them inside. Maintain a minimum temperature of 13°C.

It's still not too late to pot up prepared bulbs for forcing during this month. Select firm, healthy bulbs and plant them in large pots or decorative bowls filled with bulb fibre. Do not plant them too deep, though; keep their necks just above the compost surface. Pot up narcissus such as 'Soleil d'Or' and 'Paperwhite' for Christmas flowering.

Plunge pots after watering into a prepared bed of peat or ashes in a sheltered spot outside. Cover with polythene and check once a week or so to see if it needs watering. It's also worth potting up some of the spring-flowering bulbs purchased for the garden to be brought on early in the greenhouse. This will fill that colour gap before the first of the spring bulbs show in the garden. Try crocus, tulips, daffodils, chionodoxa, erithroniums, snowdrops, *Iris reticulata*, mascari and many more.

Overwintering

Dahlia enthsiasts will want to check over their crop this month and carefully label, low down on the plant, those worth keeping to produce cuttings next year. This roguing operation is essential to improve the stock. It's also worth colour coding the labels so that the display next year produces the whole range available.

Carefully lift and store dahlia tubers after the first frost has turned the flowerbuds black. Lift them anyway by the end of the month. Choose a dry spell so that soil is easily removed from the tubers, then cut back the main stem to about 6in (15cm). Dust dry tubers with a fungicidal powder such as 'flowers of sulphur'. Store in boxes filled with a dry peat in a well-shaded, cool, frost-free place; under greenhouse staging is ideal.

Fig 93　Label dahlias before cutting back to about 5in (12.5cm).

Fuchsias to be grown as standards next year should be selected from the crop of rooted cuttings in 3½in (9cm) pots taken earlier this year. Each will need to be caned and tied with string or wire rings. However, if the plants are to be kept growing all winter a temperature of around 10°C must be maintained.

Vegetables

Propagation

Make further sowings of lettuce. Space seed 2in (5cm) apart each way in a standard seedtray or individually into a modular seedtray filled with a peat-based sowing compost. Plant out 8–10in (20–25cm) apart in the greenhouse border before the seedlings start to touch in the seedtray.

In heated greenhouses (minimum 7°C) sow varieties like 'Pascal' and 'Revel' for maturing in early spring. There is also still time to sow varieties such as 'Ambassador', 'Magnet' and 'Kwiek' in a cold greenhouse to mature from March onwards.

Harvest the last of the tomato crop (*see also* September, page 103). If tomato plants are removed to the compost heap clear up all debris.

Pick the remaining sweet peppers if they are usable, Then remove the plants from the greenhouse.

Fruit

Harvesting

As grapes colour up they seem ripe for harvesting, but this is not the case. Depending on variety they will need to be left on the vine for at least a couple of weeks and sometimes a lot longer before they are at their best. It takes this time for the sugars to develop in the fruit. Harvesting is as easy as you make it. If you cut each bunch with a stem handling is a lot easier. Once the grapes are fully ripe they can be kept on the vine for several weeks, provided the temperature is cool and the atmosphere dry, around 7°C.

Overwintering

Peaches and nectarines now require a dry cool atmosphere to enable this year's wood to ripen before autumn. This may mean turning on heaters on damp, misty days to lower humidity and increase temperature.

Continue to water the new strawberry plants that will now be establishing themselves well in their 6in (15cm) pots. Spray the leaves each sunny morning. Discontinue watering and overhead spraying as soon as the plants start to show signs of going into dormancy. Rotting crowns can be a problem in the cold, wet winter months so it is best to move the plants to a cold frame and ventilate freely. Apply a fungicidal drench as a preventive measure.

NOVEMBER

November nearly always starts with a bang and not just on Guy Fawkes night. The weather is dominated by one Atlantic system of rainbearing clouds after another.

Chrysanthemums in the greenhouse are protected from these damaging storms and again dominate the floral display with their fabulous decorative blooms in a wide range of colours. The white and yellow forms are particularly useful as cut flowers because they brighten up the short, dull days of autumn. Perpetual-flowering carnations also have their place with their continual production of double blooms in a variety of shades all month.

Greenhouse Briefing

Restrict ventilation and give careful watering.
Check heaters regularly.
Annual greenhouse clean-up campaign.

Flowers

Label chrysanthemums.
Pot up *Iris reticulata* and *Helleborous niger*.

Vegetables

Blanch chicory and seakale.
Lift rhubarb crowns for forcing.
Sow lettuce for continuity of supply.

Fruit

Prune vines once dormant.
Ventilate peaches, nectarines and strawberries.

General Management

Cold, damp days and long nights means that cautious watering and ventilation are essential. Keep ventilators closed at night, only opening roof vents during warm sunny days when there is little wind. Again, restrict ventilation to the period around midday making sure that they are shut down a couple of hours before dusk to trap as much of the sun's free energy as possible.

Artificial heaters will be needed more often as the month progresses. For the majority of over-wintered greenhouse plants, maintain a night temperature of around 7°C and a daytime one of about 12°C, on those rare sunny days ventilate above 20°C.

Automatic vents can be a problem when you want to close down the greenhouse a couple of hours before dusk so this is a good time to disconnect and service them. Automatic watering should also be disconnected if not already done and then cleaned and packed away for the winter. Any remaining shading should be removed and glass cleaned thoroughly to allow all available light to penetrate the greenhouse.

It is important to give your greenhouse a thorough clean once a year and the quiet days of autumn provide the ideal opportunity. Pack up all the empty pots and seedtrays and move them out of the greenhouse. Choose a mild, sunny day when there is little or no wind. Take plants out of the greenhouse one by one, cleaning them up as you go and removing any dead and dying leaves. Prune if necessary. Place each pot in a sheltered spot. If the plants are particularly precious or particularly vulnerable take them indoors.

Once all the plants you wish to keep have been removed safely, it's time to start on the rubbish. Clear everything out, piling bits into plastic sacks or a wheelbarrow, and dump it on the compost heap, having first removed dead plants, old growing bags and any other debris. Separate any non-compostable stuff out and consign it to the dustbin. Then go around the empty greenhouse and pick off any bits of string from overhead wires, before scrubbing the entire structure with a stiff brush. Scrub down staging and shelving with a diluted horticultural disinfectant. Make certain all joints are cleaned out. Wash down the glass inside and out to remove algae and other dirt to allow maximum light penetration. Pay particular attention to the grime that accumulates in glass overlaps.

Replace rotten timbers in wooden-framed greenhouses — usually associated with algae growth around joints. Clear out gutters and wash seedtrays and pots. Aluminium frames should be rubbed down with wire wool or a stiff brush to dislodge dirt from aluminium sections.

Choose one of the water-based, plant-safe preservatives to treat the wood staging in the greenhouse structure, including any shelving. A couple of coats may be necessary if it has been neglected for a long time. Replace sagging wire and cracked panes of glass. Then clean out the runners of sliding doors and oil the bearings and hinges. Dig over the border soil and remove any missed debris, then water with a soil sterilant.

While the greenhouse is empty it's an ideal opportunity to put up insulation without all the usual fuss (see also December, page 114). Finally, return plants when it is safe to do so.

Flowers

Overwintering

Chrysanthemums in outdoor beds will be well past their prime and it's time to select stocks for taking cuttings from next year. Carefully label each plant as near to the ground as possible, then lift and cut each stem down to about 4in (10cm). Choose a dry spell to tease soil away from roots, then place in deep boxes filled with peat. Keep these in a cool spot — under staging in a cool greenhouse is ideal — until the next spring.

Chrysanthemums will survive the winter outside in the beds, provided they don't get too wet, but for best results take new cuttings each spring from the overwintered selected stocks.

Reduce the watering of many greenhouse plants as growth slows. Just give them sufficient water to stop the leaves wilting.

Planting

Iris reticulata and some of the dwarf daffodils can still be potted up for an early spring show (see also September, page 102).

Fig 94   Begonia Rex.

Try potting up a few crowns of lily-of-the-valley for their arching flower stems of dainty white bell-flowers. Keep them just frost-free for an early display to brighten up winter rooms. Pot about twelve good-sized crowns in a 6in (15cm) pot with a potting compost. Provide plenty of drainage.

Keep pots in a cool, but frost-free, greenhouse or frame through November and December, bringing them into a warm greenhouse or room in January. Watering should be carried out with utmost care. Do not splash leaves or tubers and crowns, otherwise you run the risk of encouraging botrytis. Liquid feed actively growing pot plants every ten days of so and try to maintain good light to prevent plants becoming leggy.

Lift and pot up roots of Christmas rose, *Helleborous niger*, to get early blooms — perhaps even on Christmas day. Don't put them straight into a warm greenhouse, though. Make a temporary stop for a few days in a cold frame.

Pots of bulbs plunged in outside beds can be brought into a cool greenhouse when shoots are 1in (2.5cm) high. Water sparingly.

Space out young plants carefully on the greenhouse staging so that they receive as much light as possible.

Vegetables

Propagation

Continue lettuce through the winter by sowing further batches of 'Columbus' and 'Kellys' in a heated greenhouse (minimum 7°C). Space seed 2in (5cm) apart each way in a standard seedtray or place individually in a modular seedtray filled with a peat-based sowing compost. When seedlings have filled the space in the seedtray, plant out in the greenhouse border about 10in (25cm) apart.

Forcing

Dig up chicory roots from sowings made last May when the larger leaves have died down leaving just the immature heart leaves. Remove sideshoots and cut back foliage to within 1in (2.5cm) of the root. Select roots with at least 1in (2.5cm) crowns, but no larger than 2in (5cm) and pot up three in a 6in (15cm) pot filled with sandy loam-based compost. The remaining roots which are useful for forcing should be stored in a cool, but frost-free place. Pot up a batch every couple of weeks for a continuous supply of crisp subtle-flavoured chicons all winter long. To force chicons it is important to exclude light; this is usually achieved by inverting an empty 6in (15cm) pot on top of the potted roots. Maintain a temperature of around 12°C to have succulent shoots in about four weeks. Cooler temperatures just mean a longer forcing period. Cut chicons when 4–6in (10–15cm) long. A root cannot be forced more than once.

Rhubarb crowns for forcing can be lifted later this month and left to get frosted on the soil surface. Box up crowns filled with moist peat and covered in black polythene to keep the light out. Check once a week or so to see the compost remains moist.

Fruit

Pruning

Leaf fall usually occurs this month and spells the time for the winter pruning of grape vines. Make sure the vine is completely dormant before you start, by cooling the greenhouse right down through generous ventilation. A dormant vine avoids the problems of bleeding shoots after pruning.

Cut back all the current season's growth to within two buds unless it is required to replace older rods or to extend existing ones. All supporting wires should be cleaned up and replaced where necessary.

You can keep the fruit of some varieties of grape vine for several weeks after harvesting. 'Lady Downe's Seedling' for instance, will last until Christmas, though only if the stem is placed in water.

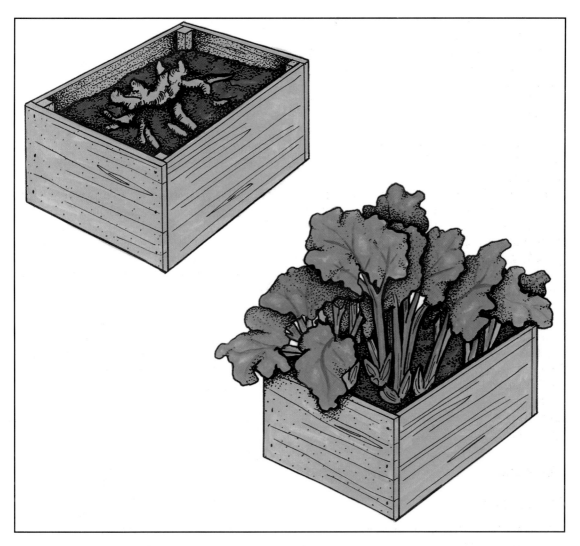

Fig 95   Place the crowns close together in a crate filled with moist peat to have a box of succulent pink rhubarb sticks at your disposal.

Overwintering

Ventilate peaches and nectarines freely on dry days to ripen the current year's wood and keep the temperature down. Don't let the temperature drop too low at night, though.

Strawberries will remain dormant from around the beginning of November to January, when they are taken into the greenhouse and started off. If strawberries are in a cold frame they must be kept well ventilated.

DECEMBER

The coldest winter weather usually waits until after Christmas before taking a grip, so December is usually the last chance to protect those not-so-hardy specimens in the garden. Lift a supply of root vegetables, too, and keep in store just in case it's a cold winter.

Greenhouse Briefing

Cautious watering and ventilation.
Insulate the greenhouse.
Light levels are critical.

Flowers

Sow *Campanula isophylla*.
Cut back greenhouse chrysanthemums.
Water calceolarias, cinerarias, cyclamen and primulas carefully.

Vegetables

Harvest plump white chicons from forced chicory.
Continue to sow a succession of lettuce for continuity of supply.

Fig 96 Bubble polythene insulation gives significant fuel savings.

Fruit

Complete winter pruning of grape vine.
Top-dress peaches and nectarines.
Ventilate freely.

General Management

Cautious watering and ventilation should be continued. Shut down ventilators at night, only opening them on sunny days. Again, maintain a minimum temperature of 7°C at night and around 12°C during the day for the majority of greenhouse plants.

Wash down the greenhouse and remove all debris, if not already done.

It is probably worth insulating any greenhouse that is heated during the winter months. Deciding what type of greenhouse insulation to buy depends to a large extent on the temperature lift required: that is, the difference between inside and outside temperatures.

The simplest form of insulation is polythene sheet. This can be attached to the greenhouse structure using pins on wood or special clips on aluminium. The idea is to create a still, insulative layer of about ½in (1.25cm) between the side of the glass and the polythene sheet. If sheets are not properly joined together or tend to move with the breeze then much of the insulation effect is lost.

For very leaky greenhouses it's best to plump for the more expensive, but more effective, bubble polythene. However, this again must be put up properly to gain the maximum benefit. This type of plastic double glazing does reduce light levels a little, but not too drastically.

One of the major restrictions to greenhouse gardening in the winter months is light. If you heat your greenhouse up too much there is a real chance of plants producing weak spindly growth because of lack of light. This can be a particular hazard with early sown crops like pelargoniums and tomatoes. Many lights are available for the greenhouse to supplement existing light and to extend day length.

Fig 97   Prayer Plant 'Maranta'.

Flowers

Cuttings

Perpetual-flowering carnations can be reproduced from cuttings this month. Don't select shoots too near the top or the base of the plant. Take 3in (7.5cm) cuttings – snapped cleanly out of the parent plant. Trim them up using a sharp knife and dip the cut end in hormone rooting powder. Stick cuttings around the edge of a 3½in (9cm) pot filled with gritty compost.

Chrysanthemums, too, can be propagated as soon as suitable material is being produced by the stocks. Select basal shoots around 3in (7.5cm) long; wait until shoots are around 4in (10cm) long before taking cuttings to leave a 1in (2.5cm) snag that will rapidly produce another batch of shoots. Trim cuttings to just below a leaf joint, remove lower leaves and dip cut ends in hormone rooting powder. Again, position them around the edge of a 3½in (9cm) pot or individually in a modular seedtray filled with a gritty cuttings compost.

Overwintering

Once chrysanthemums have finished flowering in the greenhouse and are carefully labelled cut back to about 6in (15cm) and carefully remove the debris. Light and air will then get down to the crown to encourage basal growths.

Christmas cactus should be kept moist and fed once a week with a weak liquid fertilizer. Do not move the plant once it has budded up, otherwise you risk bud drop. Also keep it away from draughts and water to prevent too dry a compost as this has the same effect.

Cyclamen will be flowering this month. They are particularly vulnerable to rot, so careful watering from below is a must. Regularly remove dying leaves and flowers by giving a sharp tug at the base of the stem.

Forced bulbs will need to be brought in from plunge beds at the beginning of the month if they are to be ready for Christmas. Some folk like to sow grass seed around the bulbs to complete the decorative effect.

Feed pot plants like calceolarias, cinerarias and primulas with a high potash fertilizer to encourage flowerbud production.

Fruit

Complete winter pruning of grape vines if this has not already been done (*see also* November, page 112). Clean up the greenhouse and scrape away at the loose flaky bark on the vine. Don't get carried away, but take it down to the smooth, brown bark underneath. Take care not to damage the buds though. Removing the loose bark will reduce the pest and disease problems for next year by either spoiling their winter hideaways or, more importantly, exposing those already hidden to an insecticide. Paint on an insecticide containing malathion for best results.

Remove the top inch or so of compost from the surface around fruit in the greenhouse and replace it with fresh loam. Dust on some sterilized bonemeal and sulphate of potash. Ventilate freely all month in order to keep temperatures down.

CHAPTER 7

Pests and Diseases

DEALING WITH PESTS AND DISEASES

The greenhouse must seem like paradise to many pests and diseases – all that lush, green growth in a warm and inviting environment makes a veritable Garden of Eden. Lack of competition and perfect growing conditions are as much of an advantage to pests and diseases as to the plants being grown, so some form of protective measures must be take to combat this ever-present threat of invasion.

Prevention is far better than cure when it comes to pests and diseases. This can be achieved to a large extent by simple hygiene, by keeping the greenhouse and its contents clean and tidy and removing any dead or dying plant material as soon as it is noticed before becoming infected.

Giving the greenhouse a thorough wash and brush-up during the less hectic winter months will reduce any carry-over problems from one season to the next. In addition, judicious watering and ventilation during the growing season will go a long way to preventing infection as well as restricting the spread of any pest or disease that has already gained a foothold.

During the growing season check all plants regularly for the first signs of pest and disease attack. If control measures are taken early, then fewer sprays of noxious chemicals will be necessary and little damage will have been caused.

Ants

Identification Small brown social insects that form colonies.

Crop Indiscriminate attackers of a range of pot-grown plants and crops in border soils.

Damage Their industrious nest-building activities can literally undermine root systems, causing the soil to become spongy. Furthermore, they farm aphids and scale insects like cattle so they can be 'milked' for their honeydew – a sugary substance these sap-sucking insects produce. Ants carry such pests onto unaffected plants to establish new colonies.

Treatment Infested pot-grown plants should be put into a bucket of water to soak overnight. Ant activities around the foundations and central pathway can be discouraged with boiling water. Alternatively, proprietary ant powders or poisonous baits containing borax can be laid down for the ants to carry back to their nest.

Aphids

Identification Small green and black sap-sucking insects more commonly known as greenfly or blackfly.

Crop Almost all plants are susceptible.

Damage Colonies of aphids will reduce plant growth rates through their sap-feeding activities and rapidly reproduce to overwhelm new growth. It has been said that if one aphid (they are hermaphrodite) was given an unlimited food supply for a whole year its offspring, in their countless generations, would outweigh the population of China – such is their rate of reproduction!

Aphids produce a sugary excretion called honeydew that is often colonized by a blanketing sooty mould fungus. They also transmit virus diseases from one plant to another.

Treatment The most effective method is to fumigate the greenhouse with a smoke cone. Alternatively, spray with a contact or contact and systemic insecticide containing either malathion, dimethoate, pirimicarb or permethrin. Very small attacks early in the season can be washed off with soapy water. Routine chemical sprays may be necessary later in the season. Try to vary the chemical used so that this pest cannot build up a resistance.

Caterpillars

Identification Long, soft-bodied grubs that are the larval stage of butterflies and moths.

Crop Different caterpillars attack various plants.

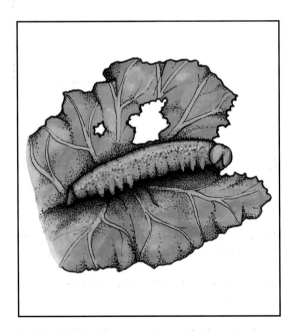

Fig 98 This small cabbage white caterpillar consumes leaves.

Damage They are avaricious consumers of leaves and sometimes fruits, producing large holes and depositing tell-tale black droppings. The carnation tortrix moth also produces webbing, holding leaves together. Flowerbuds may also be attacked.

Treatment Prevent adults entering the greenhouse by netting vents and the doorway. Individual grubs can be picked off by hand and disposed of. Attacks *en masse* can be dealt with using a gamma HCH smoke or by spraying a contact insecticide containing either permethrin, fenitrothion or rotenone (derris).

Earwigs

Identification Very common medium-sized brown insect that has distinctive pincer-shaped tail.

Crop Mostly confined to ornamental shrubs like chrysanthemums, clematis, roses and dahlias.

Damage Usually found in dry spots where they attack and disfigure the blooms and young leaves. Their night-time forays result in ragged petals and leaves, making blooms unsightly.

Treatment Trap pests in inverted pots stuffed with newspaper or straw; matchboxes also prove effective. Each morning seal the traps, remove from the greenhouse and drop the contents into boiling water. Chemical control is gained by applying gamma HCH insecticide powder.

Eelworms

Identification Very thin, almost transparent, microscopic worms. They are difficult to see with the naked eye.

Crop Attack chrysanthemums, ferns, tomatoes and daffodils.

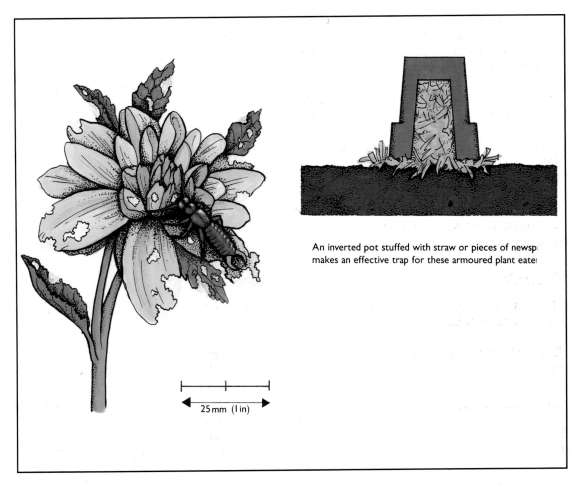

An inverted pot stuffed with straw or pieces of newsp:
makes an effective trap for these armoured plant eater

25 mm (1 in)

Fig 99 Earwigs are destructive to ornamental plants but traps are very effective.

Damage Eelworms live inside the tissue where their rapid reproduction will cause loss of vigour. Chrysanthemum and fern eelworms cause lower leaves to yellow and go blotchy, eventually turning brown. On chrysanthemums small flower-buds that develop are often disfigured. On other plants they cause leaves to distort and cysts to form on roots.

Treatment Remove and destroy badly affected plants. Chrysanthemums stools can be given hot water treatment (46°C) – dipped for about five minutes. Sterilize infected soil or replace with fresh. Growing bags may be the answer to badly infected borders.

Fungus Gnats

Identification Tiny springing flies on and around compost that are just visible to the naked eye.

Crop Anywhere there is wet compost these flies thrive.

Damage The larval stage causes a little damage attacking roots, but it is not in any way serious

119

and not worth controlling. Adults are annoying, though, so control is often sought.

Treatment Keep compost less wet; and you could try watering from beneath. Very severe attacks can usually be successfully controlled with an insecticide.

Leafhopper

Identification Like aphids these pests are also sap-sucking, but jump away when disturbed.

Crop Attack a wide range of plants.

Damage Check the undersides of mottled leaves for the skin casts they leave behind. Rarely a real problem but, like aphids, can transmit viruses.

Treatment Chemical control can be gained by spraying with a contact or contact and systemic insecticide.

Leaf Miner

Identification Minute pale green larvae of various species of fly; hatch from eggs laid just beneath the surface of the leaf. Easily identified by the damage they cause.

Crop Tomatoes, chrysanthemums, cinerarias and others.

Damage Intricate brown and creamy patterns on the leaf's surface are caused by the burrowing larvae. This disfigures the leaf and in very severe attacks reduces vigour. Sometimes rather than rambling tunnels, small brown blisters can develop.

Treatment Control individual grubs by stabbing them with a pin or the point of a penknife. Otherwise cut off affected leaves and burn. Where a single plant is badly attacked remove and destroy it.

Fig 100 The leaf miner attacks exactly as its name suggests – the burrowing larvae weave intricate patterns on the leaf's surface.

Leatherjackets

Identification Large greyish-brown soft-bodied grubs that live in the soil. They are the larvae of the cranefly or daddy-long-legs.

Crops This will attack anything grown in the border soil.

Damage This pest attacks the root system, causing plants to turn yellow and wilt. Severe attacks can kill the plants.

Treatment Mix an insecticide containing carbaryl and rotenone (derris) into the border soil when it's cultivated. Net vents to prevent adult craneflies entering the greenhouse in the first instance.

Mealy Bugs

Identification Small white, oval insects like miniature woodlice covered in a waxy woolly-looking secretion. They colonize leaf axils and leaf bases.

Crop Attack almost any permanent plant in the greenhouse, but particularly prevalent on vines, ferns, palms and figs.

Damage Again a sap-sucking insect that reduces vigour and exudes sticky honeydew, often colonized by debilitating sooty mould.

Treatment Isolated attacks can be treated with methylated spirit applied using a small paintbrush or swab of cotton wool. Treat severe attacks with a systemic insecticide containing malathion or dimethoate.

Biological Control A species of ladybird called *Cryptolaemus* feeds on mealy bugs. Adults lay eggs in mealy bug colonies and the predatory larvae of the ladybird soon bring pests under control. Works best at temperatures over 21°C.

Millipedes

Identification A worm-like multi-legged creature that, unlike a centipede, has two legs per body segment.

Crop Attacks many greenhouse plants, but particularly those with bulbs, tubers or corms.

Damage This pest usually feeds on decaying matter, but will attack roots if food sources are in short supply. It also tunnels into bulbs and feeds on tubers and corms and usually enlarges initial attacks by other pests or diseases.

Treatment Dust bulbs and corms with gamma HCH to give some protection, but soil or compost sterilization may be necessary in bad attacks.

Red Spider Mite

Identification Minute reddish-brown and fawn mites can be seen on the undersides of leaves. First signs of attack are usually the tiny white or yellow pin pricks on the upper surface that result from sap-sucking activity beneath. Webbing over leaves and stem are an easily recognizable sign of an established colony.

Crop Tomatoes, cucumbers, carnations, vines, peaches, and many more greenhouse plants.

Damage Leaves produce mottled effect, then yellow, causing loss of vigour. Eventually both leaves and blooms turn brown and die.

Treatment Since these pests thrive in warm, dry conditions, prevention is possible by encouraging a cooler, more humid, atmosphere. Spraying with chemicals has a limited effect, but a fortnightly treatment with an insecticide containing malathion, rotenone (derris), pirimiphos-methyl or dimethoate can help. Try to vary the chemical used so that this pest cannot build up a resistance.

Biological Control Introduce predatory mites (*Phytoseiulus persimilis*) in early summer. Reintroductions later in the season may well be necessary. Predators are available from specialist suppliers.

Scale Insect

Identification Inconspicuous flat brown scales found on stems and leaves.

Crop Grapes, peaches, citrus, figs and many other greenhouse plants.

Damage Sap-sucking insects weaken the plant, reducing vigour. If left unchecked the sheer numbers will eventually kill the host. Honeydew excreted by these pests can cause a secondary infection of blanketing sooty mould fungus.

121

Treatment   Isolated attacks can be treated with methylated spirit as with mealy bugs. For more severe infestations fortnightly sprays with a systemic insecticide will control immature stages of the pest's cycle. Several treatments will be necessary.

Slugs

Identification   A well-known soft-bodied pest. If not visible then look for the distinctive slime trail early in the day.

Crop   A particular problem with seedlings of almost any crop as well as the soft green growth of more mature plants.

Damage   Eat large holes in leaves, stems, shoots and roots.

Treatment   Beer traps work well; bury a cup or a bowl up to its rim in the border soil and fill with beer. The beer-swilling pests are attracted to the edge and fall in the trap.

Thrips

Identification   These very small brown insects are commonly called thunder flies. When disturbed these pests move away quickly from the plant.

Crop   Thrips are most prevalent on carnations and chrysanthemums, but they will also attack other plants.

Damage   Often abundant in flowers and on leaves where they suck sap, causing mottling of leaves. Severe attacks result in disfigurement of petals and leaves as they develop.

Treatment   Keep atmosphere moist to prevent this pest. Severe attacks can be controlled by fumigating with a gamma HCH smoke cone.

Fig 101   Slugs and snails are common garden pests; they eat soft green growth.

Alternatively, spray with a systemic insecticide containing either permethrin, pirimiphosmethyl, malathion or rotenone (derris).

Vine Weevils

Identification   White wrinkled grubs about ½in (1.25cm) long with distinctive brown head.

Crop   This pest will attack almost any pot plant as well as vines and peaches.

Damage   The grubs eat roots, crowns, corms and tubers of primulas, begonias, cyclamen and many others. The adult will also attack the edges of leaves.

Treatment   Dust gamma HCH around crowns, corms and tubers to protect them from the larvae. It is not worthwhile trying to combat the adults.

Whitefly

Identification   Small large-winged flies that can be found spreading rapidly on the undersides of leaves of affected plants. They form large colonies that all fly up together in a white cloud when disturbed.

Crop   Tomatoes, cucumbers, chrysanthemums, fuchsias and many more plants.

Damage   As a sap-sucking insect it reduces vigour and yield of fruit crops. It must be dealt with very quickly because it has a tremendous rate of reproduction and so can soon cause serious problems. It also exudes honeydew that can be colonized by sooty mould.

Treatment   Spray with systemic insecticide containing permethrin. Several sprays may be necessary to gain control. Other chemicals that

Fig 102   An example of a vine weevil larva and adult.

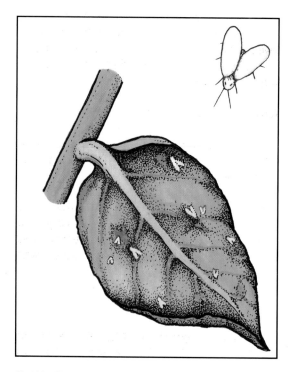

Fig 103   The sap-sucking whitefly.

give some control include those containing either primiphos-methyl or malathion.

Biological Control   Introduce *Encarsia formosa*, a parasitic wasp that lays its eggs into the larvae or scales of the whitefly. Scales turn black and another parasite wasp emerges. Subsequent generations soon gain control.

Woodlice

Identification   Grey-brown, hard-coated insects that look rather like miniature armadillos and thrive in cool, damp, shady spots.

Crop   Cucumbers, tomatoes and some other crops.

Damage   These pests feed at night nibbling at roots, stems and leaves. In severe cases plants can wilt and keel over.

Treatment   Remove all debris from the greenhouse and a good programme of hygiene should eliminate them. Problem infestations can be controlled by dusting with an insecticide containing gamma HCH or primiphos-methyl.

Botrytis

Identification   A fluffy grey mould that will appear on leaves, stems, flowers and fruits. It is usually a secondary infection gaining a foothold on damaged tissues.

Crop   Will attack a wide range of plants but the soft fleshy growth on cucumbers, tomatoes and melons is particularly vulnerable.

Damage   As a secondary infection it develops most rapidly in cool, humid conditions where there is little or no ventilation. It gains entry through open wounds from pest attack, when faded flowers fall and by pruning or harvesting cuts. Infected plants will rot and die if left.

Fig 104   An example of botrytis.

Treatment Good ventilation, generous air movement will stop the spread of the disease. Make sure you don't overcrowd the greenhouse, and pay particular attention to hygiene during the winter months when this disease is more difficult to cope with.

Remove diseased growth with a sharp knife and paint pruning wounds with a fungicide. Chemical control can be gained using a fungicide containing benomyl or a smoke containing tecnazene.

Blossom End Rot

Identification Brown, sunken, circular patches form on the blossom end of the developing tomato fruits.

Crop Tomatoes.

Damage A fruit development disorder results from an induced calcium deficiency caused by insufficient or irregular watering.

Treatment Attention should be given to the feeding and watering programme for your tomatoes.

Blotchy Ripening

Identification Fruits ripen unevenly producing mottled colours of greens, reds and yellows.

Crop Tomatoes.

Damage Renders affected fruit unappetising, caused by a nutrient deficiency in the compost. A shortage of nitrogen or potash is associated with high greenhouse temperatures.

Treatment Ventilation and a liquid feed will overcome this problem.

Damping Off

Identification A disease of seedlings in seedtrays or just after pricking out. Seedlings keel over with dark brown or black colouring at soil level. Sometimes small groups of seedlings topple in one area of a seedtray and sometimes several trays full of seeds succumb.

Crop Almost any seedling.

Damage Basal rot of seedling stem causes it to keel over and die. Disease thrives in a humid atmosphere.

Treatment Prevention is the only answer. Use well-sterilized compost and seedtrays only. Sow seed thinly and keep developing seedlings well ventilated. Where disease occurs water with 'Cheshunt Compound'.

Powdery Mildew

Identification White dusting on youngest shoots and leaves. Edges of leaves may curl under.

Crop Not fussy what greenhouse plants it attacks.

Damage Affected tissues will eventually turn yellow and shrivel. Most prevalent in hot, dry seasons.

Treatment Keep air circulating and the temperature down by means of careful ventilation, with frequent damping down to increase humidity. Spray regularly with fungicide such as benomyl immediately first signs of attack are noticed.

Rust

Identification Tiny orange-brown pinhead spots form on the undersides of leaves and release a cloud of spores when disturbed.

Crop Can affect pelargoniums, fuchsias, carnations, chrysanthemums and others.

Damage Not a common problem, but if it occurs rust can have a disastrous effect on crops, so prompt action is necessary.

Treatment Destroy badly infected plants, then spray others (not fuchsias) with a fungicide containing bupirimate and triforine. For sensitive fuchsias use the less effective thiram-based chemicals.

Tomato Blight

Identification Large, dark brown patches on leaves, stems and fruit.

Crop Tomatoes.

Damage Spots increase in size and number to cover, whole leaf and eventually whole plants cease to grow.

Treatment Choose resistant varieties. Prevent a stagnant atmosphere by good ventilation and spray the crop at fortnightly intervals with benomyl or thiophanatemethyl or copper compound. When an outbreak occurs, fumigate the greenhouse at the end of the season before removing and destroying the plants.

Viruses

Identification Various forms of leaf distortion, yellowing and mottling result from infection.

More than one virus may infect a plant at the same time.

Crop A large range of greenhouse plants are susceptible.

Damage Growth becomes weakened with an associated loss of vigour. Distortion of leaves can make plants unattractive and produce misshapen flowers.

Treatment Root out all affected plants. The control of sap-sucking insects that spread viruses is the only effective way of keeping your greenhouse free.

Wilt

Identification Wilting of lower leaves during the day (they often recover at night) is the first sign.

Crop Carnations and tomatoes.

Damage Recovery of wilting leaves is only temporary. They eventually discolour and drop – starting at the base and slowly progressing up the plant.

Treatment Remove and destroy the affected plants. Sterilize the soil thoroughly before the next crop. Choose wilt-resistant varieties when replanting tomatoes. Best of all, change to growing in bags or containers.

Index